THE
GUINEA-PIGS

By the same author

THE
GUINEA-PIGS

Britain's First Paratroop Raid

by

`Raymond Foxall

ROBERT HALE · LONDON

356674

940.5421

Photoset in North Wales by
Derek Doyle & Associates, Mold, Clwyd.
Printed in Great Britain by
St Edmundsbury Press, Bury St Edmunds, Suffolk.
Bound by Woolnough Bookbinding Limited.

Contents

Illustrations

Author's Note

This is the true story of Britain's first-ever raid on enemy territory by paratroopers, a force then in its infancy. They were the guinea-pigs used to attempt something until then never visualized – a deep penetration by airborne troops into enemy country.

On the night of 10th February 1941, just thirty-five men, the first trainees in a new art of war, dropped from RAF bombers over the snow-capped peaks of the Italian Apennines, sixty miles inland.

That it was one of the most daring raids of the war was only one of its fascinating aspects. The men were a mixed bag of Regulars and soldiers who not long before had been civilians. All were volunteers – for training as parachutists and for the first mission. Of the perils facing them when cheerfully they set out, they guessed only one – that there was no way back. It was out of what they suffered that the decision was made to go ahead with the paratroop brigades which later in the war were used with outstanding success.

The raid by 'X' Troop, No. 2 Commando, their trek over high, snow-girt mountains in a hopeless bid to escape, and the privations they experienced afterwards, form one of the hitherto little-known epics of the Second World War.

R.F.

The members of 'X' Troop, No. 2 Commando, who took part in
'Operation Colossus'

Major T.A.G. Pritchard
Captain C. Lea
Captain G. Daly
Lieut. A. Deane-Drummond
Second Lieut. G. Paterson
Second Lieut. G. Jowett
Flight Lieut. Lucky
Sgt. P.P. Clements
Sgt. A.L. Lawley
Sgt. J. Shutt
Sgt. E.W. Durie
Sgt. J. Walker
Cpl. P. Julian
Cpl. J.E. Grice
Cpl. P. O'Brien
Cpl. D. Fletcher
L/Cpl. R.B. Watson
L/Cpl. D.H. Boulter

L/Cpl. D.E. Jones
L/Cpl. H. Pexton
L/Cpl. H. Tomlin
L/Cpl. J.E. Maher
L/Cpl. D. Henderson
Tpr. J. Nastri
Tpr. A.B. Ross
Tpr. E. Samuels
Tpr. E. Humphreys
Tpr. F. Picchi
Tpr. J. Parker
Tpr. A. Parker
Tpr. D.L. Struthers
Tpr. G. Pryor
Tpr. D.J. Phillips
Tpr. J.W. Crawford
Tpr. R. Davidson

CHAPTER ONE

Zero Hour

Major Trevor Allan Gordon Pritchard wedged himself into a corner of the cavernous 'passenger' compartment of the RAF Whitley bomber and, with his back resting on the inside of the fuselage, made himself as comfortable as possible in the circumstances. He put on the earphones which would keep him in contact with the pilot preparing for take-off in the forward flight cabin, pulled the smock (then known as a jumping-jacket) straight over his battledress, reached back to adjust the lie of the parachute to which he was harnessed and settled down for the night flight and whatever lay in wait at the end of it.

Pritchard, aged thirty, was a Regular, a professional before the war began. He was big, heavily built, 5 feet 10 inches tall and weighing all of $14\frac{1}{2}$ stone, an impressive figure when he was not hunched in a corner of a Whitley. Because of the first three initials of his name, his men called him 'Tag'. But never in his hearing. You do not a call a man who has been an Army heavy-weight boxing champion, a tough rugby player and an officer for ten years anything except 'Sir' if there is the slightest chance of your voice drifting to his ears. Once it had been suggested he would be too heavy for parachuting. He had proved he was not.

Ex-public school, a peace-time military college product commissioned into the Royal Welch Fusiliers, he was a rosy-cheeked, clean-shaven type who, when he was wearing civvies, was never seen without a monocle attached to a long black ribbon. He could be described as quiet, if perhaps a little gruff. The officers under his command did not call him Tag either; they contented themselves with referring to him among themselves as "likeable" and definitely "loyal".

In the plane, listening to the pilot testing the engine thrust against the brakes, he was calm-faced, silent, thinking of nothing in the past, only of the mission that lay ahead for the unit he commanded – 'X' Troop, No. 2 Commando.

They had told him that the official name was 'Operation Colossus'. A good title, he thought. An operation of a type never attempted before in the history of the British Army must be a historic event. Truly colossal, in fact.

That was the dramatic way of looking at it. But there was, he suspected, just a little room to wonder if the tiny force he was taking into Mussolini's wartime Italy – they were just thirty-six men in all – on the night of 10th February 1941 were the subjects of a trial stunt to test the reliability, adaptability, viability and future potential of a type of unit that had never before existed in the British Army, one that had been dreamed up almost nine months before, when Britain had been cut off from Hitler's fortress Europe.

Nine months! That was the time they had been training as the British Army's first paratroops. The time of the period of gestation! Major Pritchard smiled at the thought. If this mission was only, or to a large extent, a test of what the new Army parachutists could do, then were they about to fly from this RAF base at Malta and drop into Italy to prove or disprove that the original decision to form and train a British paratroop commando was, in practice, the brilliant conception it had seemed to be when the war leader, Mr Winston Churchill no less, had ordered such a Commando to be born? Certainly they were a prototype unit. So on this trip were they, in fact, guinea-pigs?

Why was his command called 'X' troop? He knew, unofficially of course, that his men had suggested among themselves that it was 'X' for 'The unknown'. Certainly 'X' *was* used to denote an unknown quantity. Maybe they were right ...

He knew a great deal more than they did. He had been told what the target was, where it lay, what they were to endeavour to accomplish when the planes flew over it and when they floated down upon the snow-girt, moonlit mountains of southern Italy. He had also been briefed on the 'rescue' plan the masterminds of the raid had thought up to get them, it was *hoped*, out and home when the job was done, or not done, as the case might be. Whatever way one looked at it, any thought of getting them out of Italy was dramatic, ambitious.

And there was an awful lot of enemy territory to cover on foot before they reached the rescue point. For the long trek over the mountains after the job was done there was no official campaign plan forthcoming. They would be on their own.

In bare detail he had told his five junior officers, only a few minutes before boarding the planes, where to make for after the big bang and also the day – and the time – assistance was due to arrive at that point. *They* had to know in case the party became separated. But he would not tell the men.

He had, however, gone so far as to use the words 'guinea-pigs' when he had addressed the men on the runway before emplaning.

"You are pioneers – or guinea-pigs," he had said, "and you can choose which word you prefer."

Whatever reasons the High Command had for triggering off Operation Colossus, Pritchard was nevertheless proud that he and his men had been chosen for putting it into practice.

The first leg of the journey had been a flight in the same planes from an airfield in England. When they took off now from Malta, there would be no more stops. He had told them that too. This, the thirty-six now knew, was it.

One other officer taking part had known the details of the plan before this zero-hour. He was Lieutenant Anthony Deane-Drummond, and he knew only because he had been sent ahead of the troop from Britain to Malta to carry operation orders to Service chiefs there and arrange temporary accommodation for the unit during their stop-over.

Two of the remaining four officers had been infantry types before volunteering for the commando. But engineer officers would be needed on the trip, so the other two were engineers, specially trained in explosives.

There were eight bombers altogether. Six were to transport the thirty-six new-type British soldiers on their first action as paratroopers, Britain's first-ever parachute raid. In each there was one officer and five other ranks. The other two aircraft were to make diversionary bombing attacks.

The men in each plane made a last-minute check of their equipment. Each man was armed with a Service pistol and a commando knife. Slung round their shoulders were a water bottle and a haversack

x Revolver

containing food, including compressed pemmican used in the past by Arctic explorers and giving some indication of the operation on which they were setting out. Below them, ready to be dropped from the bomb racks, were containers with bren and Thompson sub-machine guns, grenades and high explosives, all attached like themselves to parachutes.

"OK, Nastri?" asked Major Pritchard. His words were addressed to the man squatting nearest to him, Trooper Nicol Nastri, a little cockney Italian who they feared would be shot as a spy for a disloyal Italian if they fell into enemy hands and his name became known. For the trip the Army Book in his pocket, therefore, showed him as 'John Tristan', an innocent English-sounding variation of the letters of his name.

"OK, sir," said Nastri.

"You've remembered that you're to stick to me like a limpet, no matter who else gets cut off from me?"

"I'll not forget, sir." The reply was in a cockney voice that could change into fluent Italian.

"Good. If we get nearer than shooting distance to the Itis, I'll need an interpreter, perhaps pretty damn quickly."

Another interpreter had arrived to join the raiding party at the last minute in England – Fortunato Picchi, aged forty-two, anti-Fascist, until then banqueting manager at London's Savoy Hotel. There had been time for him to take only one practice jump before he flew to Malta with the troop. He was a civilian in uniform with the name 'Trooper Pierre Dupont' written in an Army Book in the hope, should it become necessary, of baffling Italians about the accent with which he spoke English. "He might be useful to you," the major had told his officers. Pritchard himself was sticking to Trooper Nastri, who had been with the commando since it was formed, whom he had picked some time before and who was a soldier first and an interpreter second.

To add to the air of cloak-and-dagger secrecy with which the mission had been imbued since it was first mooted, there was another last-minute addition to the raiding party, sent to them without explanation. He bore the rather improbable name of Lucky and wore RAF uniform with flight-lieutenant's stripes and medal ribbons. Like Picchi, he looked about forty, and he too arrived at the secret base just before the troop left for Malta. Major Pritchard was informed that he spoke several languages, including Italian. Unlike Picchi, however, he was obviously well known to at least one supremo interested in the raid, Admiral Sir Roger Keyes, Chief of Combined Operations, who, when he came to the RAF take-off field to give the troop an official send-off, had a long and cordial talk with Flight-Lieutenant Lucky.

One of the soldiers on the raid, Lance-Corporal Harry Pexton, was nicknamed 'Lucky' too. Conferring with his pals, he said: "I'm the lucky one, so I think I'm entitled to say that, if Lucky is that character's real name, then I'm a Dutchman. Who could possibly have a name like that?" Names apart, however, it was obvious to every man jack that they were going to need a large slice of that commodity known as luck.

They remembered, as they climbed into their planes at Malta, that when Admiral Keyes came to see them off just four days before in England, he had said to himself in a low voice: "A pity — damned pity." The trooper standing nearest to him had heard the words distinctly. Now what did *that* mean? There was no one to ask the question of, except each other.

As the engines roared ready for take-off, the paratroop officer in one of the planes noted two men bending over another.

"What's the matter over there?" shouted Captain Gerry Daly.

"One of the men's ill, sir," came the reply. "He says he feels sick. I'd say he's got a temperature, sir."

"Well, for the love of Mike, get him off this plane," ordered Daly. "Get a door open and tell him to jump. The last thing we want on an op like this is a sick man."

Seconds before they began to move, a dark figure dropped and ran clear of the plane. Now they were down to thirty-five before they started.

Dusk was falling when the eight bombers lifted themselves off the runway and lumbered into the sky.

CHAPTER TWO

An awesome task

It had been necessary for a great deal to be accomplished before the eight bombers took off from Malta, the forward base for Operation Colossus. The operation had flourished out of a seed sown by Mr Winston Churchill within days of the fall of France to the German Army and the evacuation of British troops from Europe, known as the miracle of Dunkirk. The raid commanded by Major Pritchard had its earliest beginnings at that time.

Indeed, its story could be said to date from Churchill's ambitious foresight at a time when Britain, cut off from Europe, first prepared to defend itself from Hitler's Luftwaffe – and very probably his land forces. Churchill was not content to fight the war indefinitely with only bomber attacks from British bases, and he looked forward to a time when he hoped to mount onslaughts on the enemy in Europe by land forces. On 22nd June 1940 he sent an instruction to his Chief of Staff. To General Ismay, head of the military wing of the War Cabinet, he wrote: "We ought to have a corps of at least five thousand parachute troops. Advantage must be taken of the summer to train these forces, who can nonetheless play their part meanwhile as shock troops in home defence. Pray let me have a note from the War Office on the subject."

Two days later Major John Rock, of the Royal Engineers, a regular soldier, was asked to call at the War Office. He was informed of the Prime Minister's instruction and ordered to take charge forthwith of the military side of organizing an airborne force. It was an awesome task. No such unit had ever existed in the British Army. There was no prototype for him to study, no one in military circles to whom he could go for advice. How was he to model the force Churchill had in mind?

Parachutes were issued to RAF crews, but these were only for emergency use. Germany and Russia had trained some parachutists, but they had been little used, and in any case there was no hope of assistance from that source. No one knew anything about parachuting, except the odd daredevil who had made a parachute descent after hanging on the wing of a small biplane at a pre-war air circus. In short, Britain's knowledge of parachute descents was at worst nil and at best lamentably poor.

Consequently, Major Rock knew nothing about how to recruit or train even the nucleus of the grand force Mr Churchill dreamed of, not even how many men were to be included in the first batch of trainees. He wrote in his diary: "It was impossible to obtain information as to policy or task." What he knew even about aircraft was confined to his experience as a passenger in them. And about parachutes and parachuting – nothing. But Churchill had spoken. And for new wars new tricks.

To Rock and his contemporaries it all began as a hush-hush experiment at Ringway, some ten miles south of Manchester, where a civil airport had been taken over by the RAF after the outbreak of hostilities. The airfield was chosen because it was not near any other military operation centre; it was sited in flat rural farming country, and a flight of five or six miles in a south-westerly direction would bring a plane over an excellent 'dropping zone' near Knutsford, Cheshire – Tatton Park, the estate and country seat of Lord Egerton of Tatton. There was a large area of open parkland where the descent of trainee parachutists could be observed, and, perhaps more importantly, his lordship had given permission for his estate to be so used, though he was still in residence at the hall.

Major Rock went to Ringway, where he was delighted to find he was not on his own in the matter. Waiting there for him was Pilot Officer (later Squadron Leader) Louis Strange DSO MC DFC, a former First World War air ace, who was to organize the Air Force side of the new parachuting school.

In the spirit of secrecy that surrounded the new establishment, it was called the Central Landing School. But after Rock, by then a lieutenant-colonel, received a letter addressed to 'The Central

Laundry', and a parachute trainee, Driver Crane, got one addressed to 'The Central Sunday School', the unit was re-named the Central Landing Establishment. Humour was never far from British military matters.

Later more officers were to join the establishment's staff – Group Captain L.G. ('Stiffy') Harvey, who was to command the school, Wing Commander Sir Nigel Norman CBE, Captain Martin Lindsay (later Sir Martin Lindsay), of Polar expedition fame, and Group Captain Maurice Newnham DFC.

At first all the school was given to work on was a parachute and jumping-helmet captured from the Germans.

A staff of instructors was set up. They were mostly physical-trainer NCOs from the Army and RAF men who had been engaged in the manufacture of parachutes in peacetime. The first trainees arrived, among them the men whom Major Pritchard was to take to Italy, and when it leaked out that not one of the instructors had himself jumped from an aircraft, the situation was neatly summed up by one private soldier. "Blimey!" he exclaimed. "The blind leading the blind!"

Though that was initially true, it must be remembered that the officers and men running the school were to risk their lives many times by jumping to test methods of packing parachutes or leaving aircraft. In those early days one of them, Flight-Lieutenant Charles Agate, once jumped sixteen times in as many hours and made fourteen hundred descents helping to train parachutists. As time went on, one or two pre-war stuntmen, who had made parachute descents to thrill the crowds at air circuses, were traced and invited to join the staff at the school. Their knowledge and experience were invaluable.

Some six thousand British and Allied parachutists were trained there before the war ended. They included agents who were to drop singly into Europe, and the battalions of Allied paratroopers who made massed landings on enemy territory during the later stages of the war, including those who took part in the second-front invasion of Europe.

By then, of course, the expedition led by Major Pritchard had long been over.

How were the first guinea-pig trainees, those who jumped with Major Pritchard, attracted to Ringway? An order was sent to the COs of all

Army units asking for volunteers for a 'special service unit'. Little information was given except that those who came forward and were selected would be expected to take part in hazardous duties. The COs who pinned up the notice did not know – and the selection committees did not tell those who came forward – that the new unit would be a parachute one, and the early volunteers did not know what was to be expected of them. Throughout the remainder of the war all paratroopers were to be volunteers, the only difference being that eventually they knew what they were volunteering for.

The selection committee looked for special qualifications of physique, temperament, toughness of mind and body, determination and enthusiasm for 'having a go' at the enemy, and for men who, if the need arose, were capable of fighting alone. The one thing of which the committees could not be certain was whether a man would have the courage to make a parachute jump and go on doing so. The interviewing officers rejected three-quarters of the applicants.

It might be expected that those thus selected would be, in appearance and personality at least, of the same mould. This was far from the case, as they proved to be an individualistic lot.

First to be selected were a number of officers, including the following who later led Operation Colossus:

Major Pritchard, who grasped the opportunity of getting out of the 'tame' job of running a transit camp, which he called 'hotel keeping'.

Captain Christopher Gerald Lea, aged twenty-two, six feet three inches tall and very slim. Son of a Kidderminster mill owner, educated at Charterhouse School, trained at Sandhurst and commissioned before the war into the Lancashire Fusiliers, he was of a military family. Two of his uncles were soldiers, and his brother, later to become Lieutenant-General Sir George Lea, was then serving in India. So long as the war lasted he wished to serve in the Army, though he had thoughts later of a legal career.

He had seen active service already with the BEF in France as a brigade intelligence officer and taken part in the advance into Belgium and the retreat to Dunkirk, where he was wounded in one wrist. He was with the Territorial Battalion of the Lancashire Fusiliers in Northumberland when he learned from a fellow officer that interviews were to take place at York to recruit men for what was called a 'commando unit'. He was interviewed by Captain Peter Cleasby-

Thompson, one of the new members of the commando – and accepted. He said at the time: "I see it as a rather exciting life not unlike that of an RAF pilot – short, sharp battles with reasonable comfort between." This was a man of whom at a cocktail party in England a week before 'X' troop flew to Malta a woman said: "He has the face of a Greek god, and he should be holding a lily in his hand."

Captain Gerrard Francis Kirkpatrick Daly, Royal Engineers, aged twenty-four, was a pre-war graduate from Woolwich Military Academy and a Cambridge honours BA. His father, Sir Clive Daly, was a professional soldier knighted for diplomatic services in India during the war. His two uncles were professional soldiers in both world wars, and his twin brother, Clive, a young doctor, was later to be a parachuting MO to the 5th Paratroop Battalion. Unlike Lea, Daly was smallish, only 5 feet $5\frac{1}{2}$ inches, studious, quiet, shy, a pipe-smoker who drank very little, a man who loved immaculate clothes and fast cars. He had been in the evacuation of Dunkirk and had been described as being 'as tough as a little acorn'.

He was intelligence officer with the 5th Division in Scotland when a colonel visited the HQ to recruit for the new unit. He said only: "What we want are men who will be asked to operate in dangerous conditions." And he quipped: "I'm looking for small chaps who can get through a hole easily." He did not make it clear that he referred to the hole in the floor of a Whitley!

Lieutenant Anthony Deane-Drummond, aged twenty-three, Royal Signals, ex-Marlborough College and a Woolwich Military Academy graduate, not over-tall but burly, had also taken part in the evacuation of Dunkirk. The son of a tea-planter who had been a soldier during the First World War, and great-great-grandson of a Scots laird who lived at Megginch Castle, near Perth, in his case the saying was true that every soldier carries a brass-hat's baton in his haversack. He was eventually to become a general.

Second Lieutenant George Paterson, Royal Engineers, aged twenty-one, a Scots Canadian, born in British Columbia, every inch as tall as Lea, son of a farmer, was reading for a degree in forestry at Edinburgh University when the war began. He at once interrupted his studies to join the British Army and had just gained a temporary wartime commission when the call came for volunteers for the commando. He stepped forward because he had been assigned to chemical warfare work and feared he might spend the war in a laboratory. He was characterized as a non-regimental officer, saying to his men: "Why do you bother to keep saluting me – why don't you just look the other way?"

Second Lieutenant Geoff Jowett, newly commissioned in the Highland Light Infantry, small, stocky, almost bald, with a huge, fierce sandy moustache, like Paterson a Scots Canadian but eight years his senior and looking older than that, had come to Britain on the outbreak of war to join up. More Scottish than the Scots, in 'X' Troop he insisted on continuing to wear the Highland bonnet of his previous regiment. Again like Paterson, he was far from being 'regimental'. His method of dismissing his men was to raise a languid hand and say: "All right boys, off you go." He had been known to address his men by their Christian names and even allowed them to use his without a rebuke. Anyone who did not know him would have sworn he was an unlikely candidate for a commando unit. But when he volunteered for it he was a strong swimmer, training with limpet mines. And during training he had earned for himself the nickname 'Killer Jowett'.

CHAPTER THREE

Volunteers for hazardous duty

When the first batch of other ranks arrived at the training school on 8th July 1940, there was only one mystery they wished to solve. "What's this hazardous duty we've let ourselves in for?" they asked each other.

Two sergeants, Percy Priestley Clements, aged thirty, from the Leicestershire Regiment, and Arthur Lillian Lawley, aged thirty-five, a driving-instructor from the RASC, had a great deal in common. Both had started life as miners and later joined the Regular Army. 'Clem' Clements ("Use my Christian name at your peril") had served in India for ten years; 'Taff' Lawley had served with the South Wales Borderers in Egypt and Palestine. Taff had ended his active service, and his time on the reserve was up a month before Hitler invaded Poland, but he rejoined the Army at once. A lasting friendship, continuing through Operation Colossus, was inevitable.

Their early chats brought forward a fact that took solution of the mystery one small step forward. The officers who interviewed Clem had leaked to him that the commando, a word not in common use yet in the Services, was to be in two categories – one for airborne and the other for seaborne soldiers.

"Which would you prefer to join?" he had been asked.

"I've always wanted to fly," he replied, and that settled the matter.

Sergeant Joe Shutt, who was interviewed at the same time, had made a similar decision. They had been told in addition that applicants must be able to swim and be willing to learn to drive. But not a word was said about parachutes!

Lance-Corporal Harry Pexton, aged twenty-three, born at

Grimsby, peace-time painter by trade, only five months a soldier, characterized by a perpetual cheerfulness and accordingly dubbed 'Lucky' Pexton, chipped in: "My info's similar. I was asked which I'd like to be in – airborne or seaborne. I said I wasn't bothered which and the officer said, 'Well, I'm airborne, so I'll have you in my lot.' "

Corporal Derry Fletcher, aged twenty-two, a cost clerk, had been in the Army no longer than Pexton. He had volunteered for the Air Force when called up but was sent to the Sherwood Foresters. If he were to be 'airborne', he was partially getting his wish.

Nineteen-year-old Trooper Alan Bruce Ross, former trainee salesman, was to be the 'baby' in terms of age on the Italian operation. Called up on the outbreak of war as a Territorial Army soldier, he could trace his reason for answering the call for 'hazardous duty' to the fact that he had quite openly been 'Army mad'. His elder brother was a Regular RAF officer, and he was himself an avid reader of war books.

Corporal Philip Julian and Lance-Corporal Douglas Jones, a twenty-two-year old Devonian, an upholsterer by trade, were TA men called up at the start of the war. Lance-Corporal Jones, who was helping to man searchlights on the Devon coast, was the only one who already had an idea what the term 'airborne' meant.

"If you are selected, your duties would entail dropping by parachute," said the interviewing officer. "So if you don't wish to be chosen, you can drop out now and no one would think one jot less of you."

"Still count me in as a volunteer, sir," he had replied.

He was given a sealed letter and told to report to Tidworth on Salisbury Plain. There he was again interviewed and sent, bearing another sealed letter, to an office in London, where questions in a further interview "included some as to my political convictions". He was then given a rail warrant to Manchester but was not present when the recruits to the commando were conferring among themselves about what type of duty lay ahead for them.

Most of the soldiers in the first batch of trainees, from whom the thirty-six were chosen as guinea-pigs to drop into Italy to prove how effective in practice a paratroop section of the Army might be, the men of Operation Colossus, had until very recently been civilians. They had not had particularly exciting peacetime jobs. Only two, a speedway rider and a semi-professional boxer, had been in out-of-the-ordinary occupations. They included, apart from seasoned Regular soldiers, office clerks, teachers, salesmen, a few fishermen, some shepherds and tradesmen of different kinds. Among those who were to come later to the parachute school were professional footballers, boxers, a road cycle champion, circus acrobats, a Wall of Death rider and a male ballet dancer.

The first volunteers waited to learn what they had landed themselves with by coming to the Central Landing School. Captain Cleasby-Thompson, one of the volunteer officers to the new unit, took a roll-call of the arrivals.

"You are in No. 2 Commando," he informed them. They knew that already, and the word, not yet in common use, meant nothing to them. Then the officer said: "You are all to be trained as parachutists." He waited for the blunt statement to be partially digested and continued: "You are privileged to be the first men in the British Army to be asked to jump out of aircraft and reach the ground by the aid of parachutes. You should all feel very proud."

Not one man moved a muscle or asked a question, and it will probably never be known whether this was due to resignation or shock.

"I must warn you in the most serious manner that you are not to talk to anyone, neither Serviceman nor civilian, about this training," added the captain. "That is all."

After he had left, one wag crystallized their thoughts with the words: "That is *all*. Well, it's enough to be going on with, eh, pals?"

From that another took his cue. He said: "Just like the bloody Army to entice us into this, wait until there's nothing we can do about it – and then tell us the worst."

It was only typical Army grumbling. They had volunteered for 'hazardous duty' and they were certainly going to get it.

Despite Mr Churchill's order, there had been much opposition to the idea of the school. Some officers in the military hierarchy claimed that parachutists would be shot by the enemy before they reached the ground. Others asked how, if they did land, they could assemble quickly enough to be effective.

One senior RAF officer wrote: "There are very real difficulties in this parachute business. We are trying to do what we have never been able to do hitherto, namely to introduce a completely new arm into the Services at little notice and with totally inadequate resources and personnel.

"Little, if any, practical experience is possessed in England of any of these problems, and it will be necessary to cover in six months the ground that the Germans have covered in six years."

On the other hand Admiral Sir Roger Keyes, who as Chief of Combined Operations commanded the new seaborne and airborne commando units, believed that soldiers could go by air to battle and be effective.

The trainees at Ringway RAF Station knew nothing of these upper-strata arguments. But they were not long in realizing that the school was not only taking its first tentative steps; it was also starved of the best equipment. With fears of invasion of Britain and the RAF requiring all its aircraft for bombing raids on Europe, only four ageing Whitley Mark II bombers were handed over for parachute training. At the sight of them one prospective paratrooper was heard to gasp: "Blimey, flying coffins." The name stuck.

The instructors had not yet attempted their own descents, contenting themselves meanwhile with dropping dummies attached to parachutes and noting the results. It did not take the men long to learn that their instructors were also learners and that they themselves must be guinea-pigs. In the meantime the trainees were taught how to fall out of the door of a stationary bomber without injuring themselves. But a phrase gained popularity among the trainees: "A right lark this is – the blind leading the blind."

The method used was the same as that later for the men. The parachutes were attached to static lines hooked to a steel bar in the aircraft, so that they opened automatically as the man or load left the aircraft. One steel bar gave way, and the dummies plummeted to the ground with parachutes unopened. Another of the dummies fouled the tail of the Whitley.

Anti-aircraft commanders in the vicinity were warned that parachutists would be training in the Ringway and Knutsford areas. "They are not to be shot at," read the order.

The recruits to the commando were given pep talks suggesting that they were the fittest men in the Army, that there was nothing they could not accomplish, that they were indeed very special men. They were encouraged to believe that they were a *corps d'élite*, and if some began to adopt a swaggering personality, this was encouraged, as was also any sign of individuality and confidence.

They were to need every assistance to face what was required of them. It was realized already by the school that to jump out of an aircraft and pin one's faith on a twenty-eight-foot circle of nylon or cotton and twenty-two-foot-long lines of rigging unfolding correctly from a bag on the shoulders required an individual type of courage not necessarily akin to the utmost bravery on the field. It was anticipated that some men would funk it, but it was also realized that this would by no means denote that that man was not brave. Even among those who made their first jump unhesitatingly, it was rare if they did not have to conquer fear every time they jumped afterwards.

The day came for the first batch – those who were to fly from Malta with Major Pritchard – to attempt their first training jump. One morning in mid-July they were wakened at 4 a.m. A bus took them to the airfield, where the first six were given parachutes and told to board a waiting Whitley. Inside were a number of sergeant instructors. The doors were closed and locked.

The bomber took off, and the instructors took away the covering from a hole that had been cut in the floor of the aircraft. (This had been found to be the only suitable exit for a Whitley.) The trainees were ordered to don their parachutes, clip them to the steel bar and sit round the open hole, together with two instructors, their legs dangling through. Through the open hole the ground, a long distance below, could be seen sliding away beneath them.

"It's as simple as falling out of bed," said an instructor with a harsh parade-ground voice. "You don't do anything but jump. Nothing to pull or push. Your parachute will open by itself because it is attached to this static line. You've absolutely nothing to worry about." The voice held a note of utter confidence, perhaps more than the speaker felt, as he added: "God's honour, mates, there's nothing to it."

Over the mere and parkland at Tatton, the pilot throttled back to 100 m.p.h. and flew at a few hundred feet. One instructor dropped through, then another. Peering down, the men saw their parachutes ballooning, the human appendages dangling below, floating down like gigantic white umbrellas into the far distance below.

One of the instructors tapped a man on the shoulder. He was Ross, the youngest trainee.

"Go!" The word echoed in Ross's ear. Sitting on the rim of the hole, he pressed down hard and heaved himself through. There was a noticeable jerk on his shoulders, the canopy cracked open above him – and he was safe. He admits that, when he scrambled to his feet after landing, his first thought was that he was alive after all.

Up in the aircraft an instructor said laconically: "See? Dead easy. The youngest of you lot too, isn't he?"

There was a murmur of assent. What Ross could do they could do. No one said it. But they all thought it. Doug Jones went next, then the rest.

Other methods were used at different times. The school was given an old Bombay troop-carrier, and this had an opening in the side of the fuselage through which to leap. Lucky Pexton's first jump was executed in this way. "As I stood there at the hole waiting to jump, I knew in a blinding flash that by joining this mob I'd made the greatest mistake in my life." In his usual light-hearted style he said this to his pals. But he did not say it *before* he jumped. He said it *after* a perfect landing.

On 25th July the men filed as usual into a room at Ringway to be issued with parachutes. Some 145 descents had been made with only an odd bruise or sprained ankle to show for it.

Trooper Evans was about to take a parachute when his name was called, and as he hesitated and turned his head, Doug Jones took the one being proffered. Turning back, Evans took the next, the one Jones would normally have had. Jones made a perfect landing. He looked up. He knew Driver Evans was jumping next. He saw Evans leave the aircraft and drop – continue to drop, like a stone on the end of a string. Evans, wearing the chute meant for Jones, crashed to his death not a hundred yards away.

It was the first training fatality, and the memory of it would not be easy to erase from the thoughts of the others.

An officer was giving a talk on how safe parachuting was. A soldier arrived with a written message.

"I have some bad news for you," said the officer. "A man has just been killed."

CHAPTER FOUR

Transformed into commandos

As a result of Trooper Evans's death, all parachuting was ceased temporarily. Then the men were addressed by officers, who explained that Evans had got into a spin when the first eight feet of the parachute had left the bag and that this had wrapped round him, causing him to fall unchecked to the ground. It was, they said, "a chance in a million". No one would be asked to continue jumping until the most rigorous checking of parachutes and investigation of dropping had been made by the school's staff.

Apart from having seen the first accident occur, the men were not happy about the method of departure from Whitleys. The hole cut in the floors of them narrowed to the exit; this meant that the trainees had to be careful to drop in an upright position and push themselves from the rim with just the right force; failure to do so resulted in a painful blow in the face from the opposite side of the hole – known as 'The Whitley kiss'.

Each man had to make seven training jumps before being given a rest from them, and before they made the remainder of these, experiments were made making descents from the rear bombers. This entailed standing at the tail on a platform built virtually outside the aircraft, pulling a 'D' ring and allowing the opened parachute to jerk the trainee off the plane. It was known as the 'pull-off' method. The authorities described it as "a gentle way of introducing men to the act of parachuting". But Sir Martin (then Major) Lindsay, who experimented with descents in this way, found on the first occasion that he experienced a sort of temporary blackout. He said: "I knew a man once who said he had been paid £1 a time by the Chilean

Government for testing thirty parachutes. All I can say is that it wasn't enough – not nearly enough." Some of the men who tried it were also not enamoured with it. "It was a damned frightening experience," said one.

In fact no method in those early days was as comfortable as the men would have wished. Jumping through a door in the side of a high-winged Bombay transport, for instance, meant getting a full view of the ground far below before leaping, and the handle one clung to beforehand felt disconcertingly loose.

In the end it was the soldiers' philosophical attitude that counted. "If your number's on it, you'll buy it – it's as simple as that," they began to say. "If your luck holds, then you're OK."

Later, when much more had been learned about parachuting, the training of paratroopers became easier, and there seems little doubt that the men who flew on Operation Colossus were also guinea-pigs while being trained.

Already the minds of the commanders of the school were turning to what use the first trainees could be put to. Lieutenant-Colonel Rock investigated the special military requirements for men who were being trained to go into battle by air, while Wing Commander Norman studied methods which might be used by pilots transporting the paratroopers and dropping them for action.

The parachute 'graduates' were then packed off to Scotland, where the Lovat Scouts, prior to this time the first unit in the Army to resemble a commando-style force, were based. There Lord Lovat and his men, from their School of Irregular Warfare in a country house a few miles from Fort William, were already training the first of the seaborne commando force envisaged by Mr Churchill, and the new paratroopers were to undergo six strenuous weeks under the tutelage of the toughest of mountain men. The trainees from Cheshire did not know it then, but the Scottish mountains resembled those over which on a moonlit night they were to jump into southern Italy ...

One group of the new paratroopers remember the first task set by their instructor, a grey-haired old man who they believed had seen the best of his days. "We'll just go for a wee walk together," he told them genially. It turned out to be an arduous climb to the top of Ben Nevis, but to the old Lovat Scout NCO it was "just a wee walk".

"Don't worry Dad," quipped one of his charges. "Take your time, and we'll wait for you at the top."

On the summit *he* was waiting for *them*, smoking his pipe and scarcely out of breath. "What kept ye?" he inquired in his soft Highland voice. "Now we'll all go down and try again."

As time went on, they were taught how to climb a mountain using the least possible energy, how to come down again in the quickest time possible.

During the first week of this training, Sergeant Clem Clements admitted: "I've had a few gruelling experiences on the frontier in India, and I thought I was tough. But I lagged behind those ageing Lovat Scouts, all the way up and all the way down."

Captain Lea said: "Those men were terrific. They were certainly wise in the ways of the mountains."

"This training is for real," they were told. "You must all get used to being on your own, no matter what might occur, think yourselves what is best in a given situation, fight and survive alone if you are separated from your mates."

They were acquainted with a new order. If any man was injured during training, no one was to go to his assistance unless the injury was serious. Instead that man must get back to camp the best way he could. Self-reliance was as necessary as toughness, their officers told them, "for the action for which you are being trained". Casualties must not interfere with "the success of that future action".

On one occasion Lucky Pexton was not so lucky when he sprained an ankle near the summit of Ben Nevis. He was left to hobble and crawl seven miles to camp. He knew that the drivers of Army vehicles in the vicinity had been ordered not to stop to give any soldier a lift. "To hell with that for a tale," Pexton told himself. At the foot of Ben Nevis he hailed a passing ration lorry. It did stop, and drove him to his camp.

They were given intensive day and night training shooting with small arms and tommy- and bren-guns and throwing grenades, and given instruction in the use of explosives. They were also taught to stalk and shoot deer. "If you can stalk a deer," said the mountain men, "you can hunt a man."

They were switched to rowing whalers in a loch, swimming with full kit, route marching, cross-country running. "They never left us alone," said Lieutenant Deane-Drummond. "A day off duty meant 'just a wee run to the top of Ben Nevis'."

One day two middle-aged Scotsmen dressed in smart lounge suits arrived. One was short and portly, the other tall and slim. They seemed utterly benign old gentlemen, and when they introduced themselves as "Fairburn and Sykes" it was inevitable that a wag among the trainees was heard to suggest: "Bloody hell, now it's a ruddy music hall act." That man was soon to take back his words. Former Shanghai policemen, they had arrived to teach unarmed combat. Their expertise had been learned on riot duty, and they taught the men judo, knife fighting, how to snatch a pistol from a man before he had a chance to pull the trigger, how to kill with the back of the hand, even with a matchbox – how to kill, in fact, by fair means or foul. The knives and pistols were inside their jackets. "Remember, gentlemen," they would say, "go for the eyes, ears or testicles."

Another man dressed in civvies and wearing thick-rimmed glasses arrived to give lectures. Small, soft-voiced, studious, formerly with the International Brigade in the Spanish Civil War, he was an expert in street fighting.

This definition of the word 'commando' was published after the war:

The word was used by the Boers during the South African War of 1899-1902 and applied to a swift-moving body of mounted troops used by them against less mobile British forces. In 1940 the name was applied by the British to contingents formed to carry out special tasks during the Norwegian campaign.

After Dunkirk these contingents were re-organised into battalions and formed into raiding parties that co-operated with the Royal Navy and Royal Air Force. They were shock troops drawn from the Royal Marines and most regiments in the British Army.

A member of a commando unit was trained in unarmed combat and to be a crack shot with all types of small arms, a deadly executant with knife and bayonet, an expert in demolition work with or without explosives. He had to be capable of marching thirty miles a day over rough country in full equipment and of going into action at the end of it. He was also trained to operate independently for long periods, to live on the country and to be able to cook his own food.

Every man was required to be able to swim a specified distance in full kit and with his rifle kept above water. So rigorous was the training that only five per cent of the men volunteering for commando units reached the physical standard and military efficiency demanded.

When this first batch of paratroopers returned to Ringway in early September 1940, all had fulfilled those requirements, and it appeared that the selection committees had done their job extraordinarily well.

CHAPTER FIVE

A show for brass hats

They returned, as they had been meant to, with a swaggering pride, feeling like invincible heroes, with a fine sense of being the cream of fighting men – but to news which humbled that pride. During their absence in Scotland a man from a new intake to the commando, Trooper Watts, from the Household Cavalry, had plunged to his death in Tatton Park when his parachute failed to function properly. And Lieutenant-Colonel Rock was in hospital with severe concussion following a heavy parachute landing.

They came back, however, to some improved conditions. It had been discovered that it was safer for dropping planes to glide at no higher speed than 90 m.p.h. with the tail up. The packing bags of the parachutes had also been re-designed so that the rigging lines came out before the canopy to reduce the danger of entanglement. And parachutes were now being manufactured specially for the school. Last but not least, the school had acquired for its staff two valuable and experienced aerobatic stuntmen – Harry Ward and Bill Hire, peacetime parachutists with Sir Alan Cobham's Air Circus.

The commando's HQ was now Cliff House in the country town of Knutsford at the edge of the dropping zone, and on their return the men were billeted in the town and taken by bus to Ringway to emplane for their continued jumping practice. Nothing could now daunt their spirit of bravado. As they floated down, they tried to light cigarettes or take photographs.

There was an air of expectancy. The operation to be led by Major Pritchard was being organized in earnest. Assisting Wing Commander Sir Nigel Norman and Colonel Rock (when he returned to duty from hospital) to mastermind it were: Major Lindsay (later to be created a baronet), who had been experienced in survival techniques as a Polar explorer and who at this time wrote a paper for the Chief of the Imperial General Staff on the military aspect of German paratroopers dropped in Holland. Major J. Lander, who arrived to determine what weapons and ammunition would be suitable to be dropped for use of those taking part in the raid. Captain Bill Brandish, of the Royal Irish Fusiliers, to instruct in infantry tactics and liaise between the school and the new commando.

Group Captain Maurice Newnham wrote to High Command of the men who were to take part in Britain's first paratroop raid: "They are splendidly disciplined troops inspired by great ideals. They are physically perfect specimens capable of the greatest bodily and mental strain."

It was now necessary to practise night descents. Instructors executed the first of these – with lights fixed to them. Then they perfected dropping a stick of parachutists quickly out of an aircraft, and mock attacks were mounted on the ground.

In November it was arranged for them to put on a show on Salisbury Plain to show the High Command what they could do. They would drop near a Wiltshire village 'held' by infantry from Southern Command and attempt to 'take' it. The pilots from the school, now expert at dropping parachutists on target, placed them feet away from a row of brass-hats, who cheered as the men ran for the village.

Initiative was the order of the day. The commander of one company, Captain Cleasby-Thompson, had the audacity to commandeer a VIP limousine at pistol point and force the chauffeur to drive as many men as it would hold to the village. Similarly they took command of a lorry and forced the driver to take them into the village hidden under tarpaulin in order to surprise 'the enemy'.

The brass-hats drove into the village from the dropping zone to determine the success of the 'attack'. A staff car stopped at a pub where Corporals Pexton and Fletcher were 'on guard' in the 'captured' village. A Field Marshal stepped out. He was accompanied by Crown Prince Olaf of Norway, who asked the two paratroopers: "Are you two of the parachute men?"

"Yes, sir."

"Well, you have done very well," said the Prince, smiling, and followed the Field Marshal into the pub.

The landlady came out bearing a tray with three pints of beer – one each for the paratroopers and the third for the sergeant-driver of the staff car. "These are from Prince Olaf with his compliments," she said.

The sergeant driver fixed an eye on Pexton. "Hey, are you one of the blighters who pinched a car?"

"Yes," grinned Pexton.

"Do you know whose ruddy car it was?"

"Not the faintest idea," returned the corporal.

"Well, corp, for your information, it was his – him who went into the pub, Prince Olaf!"

"Really?"

"Yes. And my advice to you is you'd better be more careful in the future."

"Oh? Well my advice to you is you'd better look after that posh car of yours."

"Why?" inquired the sergeant.

"Because if we need another car in a hurry, we'll pinch that one as well."

The sergeant was not unimpressed with what he had seen and heard that day. He at once opened the car bonnet and immobilized the vehicle.

War correspondents were invited to witness and describe the exercise, each one being told that what was written could not be published for some time as the existence of the paratroopers was for the time being an official secret. The articles the journalists wrote that day were in fact published a year later – after Operation Colossus had taken place.

The story one of the correspondents wrote at the time – it was published later – contained these observations:

Britain's parachute troops are prepared, when the call comes, to go out on difficult and perilous missions as a new striking force of the Army, but not necessarily in the same way as enemy parachutists operated last spring in Europe.

It was a fascinating experience to see the parachute troops dropping one by one at short but regular intervals from aeroplanes which roared overhead at comparatively low altitudes.

Quantities of 'umbrellas' opened and slowly descended. All the men I saw jump landed without any difficulty, except one whose shoulders were slightly injured. In a moment they had disengaged themselves from their parachutes and advanced to take up previously planned positions.

The whole operation was carried out with a smoothness which indicated that the British Army's use of parachute troops had long passed the experimental stage.

Our parachute men are, as might be supposed, of considerable resource, initiative and daring. Some of the men who came down near me were busy 'inducing' the driver of Prince Olaf of Norway's car at bayonet point to take them across the country. The men certainly looked pretty tough.

(It is interesting to speculate on whether this journalist or any of his colleagues dreamed on that day that four years later war correspondents were themselves to parachute into France with the battalions of paratroopers who took part in D-Day, the start of the Allied invasion of Europe.)

The High Command were profoundly impressed. Now, it was decided, was the time to consider another experimental exercise – this time into enemy territory. A target must now be chosen, and the operation decided upon was to be the raid on southern Italy, code-named Operation Colossus.

Buoyed up with their success, the three dozen men returned to Ringway to learn that Corporal Carter had crashed to his death in Tatton Park. A hook had caught on the edge of the jumping-hole and caused the static line to be disconnected. The parachute had no chance of opening. Yet another modification had to be made.

CHAPTER SIX

A target is chosen

The men had proved they were ready. The big experiment was at hand. To test fully the striking power of a large future paratroop force, it had already been decided that the drop should be made into difficult rather than easy terrain, and the wild and mountainous country of southern Italy was favoured. But a precise target had to be found, and the official finger had not yet been laid upon that.

Italy showed the most promise for an experiment for another reason. Mussolini's main force was occupied fighting in Albania and North Africa, and although he had left a defensive force at home, a raid there might not be quite so suicidal as one in strongly held Nazi Europe for a first attempt to drop in on the enemy from the sky. It would be dangerous enough, however, and if the target chosen resulted in some strategic advantage, so much the better.

Before the war a civil engineering company in London had assisted in building a huge aqueduct in the ankle of Italy. This was in the province of Campagna, about thirty miles east-north-east of Salerno. It spanned a gorge through which the Tragino flowed, amid towering mountains over which the peak of Monte Vulture soared the highest. The question of a target was solved when the company suggested that it might be worth a few bombs being dropped on the aqueduct. Yes, said the War Office, it would be an excellent idea. The aqueduct carried the main water supply for the province of Apulia – and to Brindisi, Bari and Foggia where there were dockyards and military factories. It would not help the Italian war effort if those towns became short of water. Unfortunately attack by bomber aircraft in that mountainous region would be far from easy.

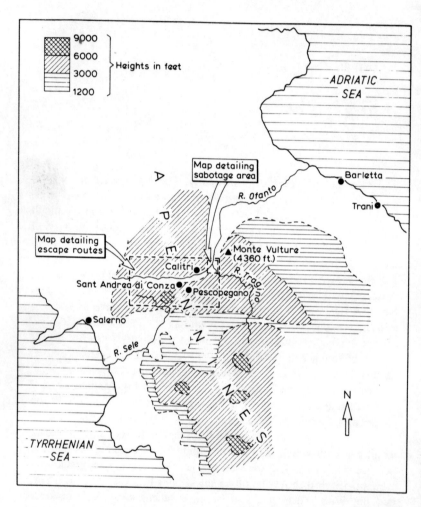

Southern Italy showing the raid area

But was this not the very target for which they were searching? It was surely just the job to give to the new paratroopers, waiting to go on the first experimental raid. An attempt could be made to drop them as near to the aqueduct as possible – and enough explosives with them to blow the thing to pieces. It would not be easy. It would be highly dangerous. But if it were to be an experiment, then let it be a really big one.

In the last days of 1940 secret talks took place between the War Office and the directors of the engineering firm, who knew a great deal about the aqueduct.

Early in January 1941 the commando were called on parade at their HQ at Knutsford, and their CO, Lieutenant-Colonel Jackson, addressed them: "An operation has been planned with the intention of penetrating deep into enemy territory. It is top secret and you are all on your honour not to speak a word of it to anyone.

"Some of you will be privileged to take part. I shall be asking for volunteers, but before I do so, I must say now that it is most unlikely that any arrangements can be made to rescue any who take part in it and who indeed survive. I must also say that, although those eventually taking part will be wearing uniform, it is likely that the enemy would look upon anyone they capture as a spy – and you know what that means.

"However, I should say that only about forty of you will be required."

The CO paused. His eyes passed over the khaki rows. Each man had undergone the full course as a paratrooper and commando. Every one had won his spurs.

"Now," he said, "will volunteers take one step forward."

It was a proud moment for Colonel Jackson. Every officer and man stepped forward. It was like a precision drill movement.

"Very well," said the colonel. "I thank you all, but I'm afraid this means the men who are to take part will have to be selected." His task was not made easier by a steady stream of men calling at the commando office to give a multitude of reasons why each should not be left out.

The officer chosen to lead the expedition was Major Pritchard, Jackson's second-in-command. He was told to pick five officers to go with him and to ask them in turn to choose five men each, of whom they would be in charge, with a few in reserve to allow for illness or injury occurring before the operation got off the ground. He would himself choose five men. There were four troops – A,B,C and D – from which to draw men and form them into a fifth troop – designated 'X'.

The new troop 'X' was taken at once from Knutsford to Ringway and given accommodation together in a large wooden hut. Until operation day they were to be kept incommunicado. The officers talked to each man individually to stress the importance of not talking to anyone, either at the station or out of it, about what was afoot.

"God knows this is going to be a difficult enough task," they said, "and if the faintest whisper got to the enemy's ears, it would be harder still."

In the evenings they were allowed to leave the station to visit a pub, only one and always the same establishment. But security men in civvies went with them and listened to their conversation to make sure not one 'dangerous' word was uttered. Their letters home were 'vetted' by officers before being posted.

In that cold January of 1941, intensive training began for 'X' Troop – thirty minutes PT before breakfast, a daily three-mile run and a fifteen-mile fast march carrying full equipment. Then there was night shooting practice with Colt automatics and sub-machine guns.

Dieticians arranged a diet for them that would build up reserves of energy. Major Lindsay asked a food firm to make special rations for them to take on the raid. These included slabs of pemmican, a concentrated meat protein which, when boiled with a little water, made a thick 'porridge' of high nourishment. Each man was to carry enough pemmican (at two pounds a day, the Polar expedition ration) to last for six days.

Meanwhile, the officers in command of the Central Landing Establishment were battling to gain the aircraft and equipment required for the raid.

"There's a shortage of operational aircraft," said the Air Ministry. "We might squeeze through for you a flight of Whitleys and Bombays."

"No go," replied Ringway. "We want all Whitleys. Good ones. We can't organize two different lots of equipment."

"Well, *we* can't lose a flight of front-line bomber aircraft *and* their crews for a matter of several weeks at a critical stage of the war. You have our sympathy," came the reply. It was always, of course, a critical stage of the war.

"Sympathy not enough," the message went back from Ringway. "How in heaven's name can we do what we've been ordered to do without the proper equipment? Will refer the matter to higher authority unless we get the best."

Group Captain Harvey went to the Air Ministry. He pointed out that the operation would have to fly a dangerous route of nearly a thousand miles to get even to their strike-base at Malta. Bombays would be more susceptible to attack by enemy fighters, he said. His point had to be taken. "This is the very first airborne experiment," he insisted, "and it won't have a cat in hell's chance with a mixed flight of aircraft." In the end he got what he wanted — eight Whitleys in first-class condition, six to carry the paratroopers and their equipment and two to make a diversionary raid on railway yards at Foggia. Wing Commander Tait arrived at Ringway with them, plus selected pilots and air crews.

In a matter of weeks the school's pilots had to pass on to Wing Commander Tait and his pilots the expertise they had learned dropping parachutists. The air crews who would transport 'X' Troop to their target were used to dropping bombs from a great height instead of men from about four hundred feet at a slow speed in mountainous country. While this was in progress, the six sections of 'X' Troop practised jumping in quick succession, assembling after landing and container collecting.

The excitement of the run up to the raid was punctured by another jumping fatality. On 22nd January Lance-Sergeant Dennis drifted too far during a descent and landed in an ice-covered pond — to drown in three feet of water due to deep mud.

A forty-foot long wooden mock-up of the aqueduct was erected in Tatton Park behind Lord Egerton's house. A guard was placed on it day and night to prevent its being seen by the public. It looked like a bridge, and the men were told only that it was 'a bridge' they were to blow up. They were not told where. The troop practised dropping and manhandling heavy containers to the bridge. Eventually they could carry weights of half a ton there in just over half an hour.

It was obvious that some sort of operation was in the wind, and many ploys were used to put people's minds on the wrong track. Maps of Abyssinia, for instance, were left on tables and shelves at Ringway. The organizers were very security conscious.

Every man of the sabotage company was taken into Group Captain Harvey's office to study a plasticine model of the area into which they were to drop. It showed to exact scale the mountains, the aqueduct over the gorge, the Tragino and its tributaries, and clumps of trees. RAF photographers had flown over the area and done their job well. Each man was told to memorize everything in the vicinity of the aqueduct, which was still referred to as a bridge, and still they were not told in which country the area was situated. Not only was the 'map' kept under lock and key; constant guard was kept on the office.

At this time the War Office told the organizers at Ringway to stand by to receive two men to join the saboteurs. One was the civilian Fortunato Picchi (literally 'Little Fortune'), suave, polite, small, rotund, Italian, a British citizen, anti-Fascist, London restaurant chief, interpreter, to be put into uniform as 'Trooper Pierre Dupont' and introduced to the troop as a Frenchman. Were they, then, to drop into France? No one provided the answer. But they were certain of one thing about their new comrade – he was as unlikely a soldier as could possibly be imagined, and if he were taken prisoner, that was what his captors would think.

The other late arrival was Flight-Lieutenant Lucky, the man with the unbelievable name, who wore First World War ribbons and must be over forty years of age. The men learned that between the wars he had worked in the Middle East, but no indication of what work he had performed there was given! He had married an Egyptian woman who spoke Italian. He was a fluent speaker of a number of languages.

His arrival added a piquant touch of mystery to the forthcoming raid.

"He's a strange fellow," confided one soldier to another. "What's *he* coming for?"

"Is the War Office taking this opportunity to get a secret agent into – whatever country we're going to?" asked another.

Neither of the questions was answered.

Some last-minute personal arrangements had been made. Precise little Picchi, on whom there was no obligation to take part, made his Will.

Captain Daly mentioned casually to the Reverend William Austwick, with whom he was billeted in Knutsford, that no one ever knew what might happen to a soldier, and if he ever went away and failed to return, he would be grateful if the clergyman would contact his twin brother, Dr Clive Daly, who was at a London hospital.

Lance-Corporal Doug Jones took a romantic step. Before the troop set off, he married a girl he had met in Knutsford, and was given three days' marriage leave, returning to the troop, as it turned out, two days before the flight to Malta.

The 'dress rehearsal' was a night drop for a final assault on the wooden 'bridge' in Tatton Park. Some minor injuries were sustained; one man was stranded on the roof of Tatton Hall, other in trees Jones, just married, landed in a midden and had to be issued with a new uniform; Major Pritchard caught a leg in his parachute rigging but extricated himself just in time. But no one was prevented from going to Malta and, as they say on the stage, if the dress rehearsal is a flop, the first night will be terrific.

On 24th January Lieutenant Deane-Drummond left Ringway unobtrusively with operation orders to fly from fog and snowstorms in England to glorious weather in Malta.

A general came to the men who were to notch up a British 'first' in operations. He had a word with every man. "My information is that you are the fittest three dozen men in the Army," he said.

Everyone knew it would not be long now. The countdown to zero had begun.

CHAPTER SEVEN

Salute to the brave – by an admiral

On 3rd February 1941 'X' Troop set off, travelling by special bus to RAF Mildenhall, Suffolk, from which airfield they were to fly to Malta. There were thirty-nine in all, including one officer and two troopers in reserve who would not go beyond Malta if the rest were all fit and well.

On the same day Wing Commander Tait and his fellow pilots flew the Whitleys there from RAF Ringway. All were confined to the camp for the three days that were to elapse before they flew on the first leg of the operation.

In this atmosphere of secrecy their battle tunics were collected. When they were returned to them, they were told that certain items had been sewn into them. In the lining of each garment there were now 50,000 lire in notes – in some cases in the collar, in others the waistband, the idea being that, if they were captured, the money might not be discovered in all cases. In the seam of cloth above the left breast pocket was secreted a small, fine hacksaw blade (a thriller-story touch here, as the blade was intended as a possible escape tool if the soldier were captured!). And in the lining of the sleeves were two one-foot-square silk maps, one of northern and the other of southern Italy. Each man was given a metal collar stud and ordered to wear it always and not lose it. "If you scrape the white paint from the back of it," they were told, "You will find a tiny compass."

The officers' tunics had ten gold sovereigns sewn into them. Why were they given a different currency? No one came up with an answer to that one, and it was assumed that the only benefit over the lire given to other ranks was that the sovereigns would hold their currency value anywhere in the world.

Flight-Lieutenant Lucky also had sovereigns in his tunic, and his fellow officers on the mission noted that he was particularly interested not only in these but also in the other items secreted in the uniforms. Their interest in him was less inquiring than that of the men, but while accepting that his job was no more than they had been told, they allowed themselves a passing thought. "This chap Lucky," they confided in each other briefly. "Strange sort of interpreter, don't you think?"

On 7th February Admiral Sir Roger Keyes, Chief of Combined Operations and responsible for commando training, arrived at the station to give the men an official send-off. The troop were paraded in the hangar with their Whitleys.

The admiral shook hands with each man and chatted briefly. It was obvious to all that his face was extremely grave. This was a man who, more than any other connected with the raising and training of this troop, strongly believed in the efficacy of parachuting soldiers into battle. Why then was he so grave? Did he have some prophetic sixth sense of just what the troop were to encounter when they jumped into Italy? Did he know that as pioneers and pathfinders every one of these men now setting out on the raid was expendable, that their job was merely to blaze an experimental trail for the paratroopers who were to follow in their wake later in the war? No one, of course, was going to ask for an answer to those questions, and in any case no answer was to be forthcoming.

The admiral spoke longer to two men than to any of the others. One was Major Pritchard, who was commanding the raid. The other was Flight-Lieutenant Lucky, with whom Admiral Keyes seemed to be acquainted already. Who precisely was Lucky? Again the troopers asked themselves the question.

Then the admiral's voice was raised as he addressed the company: "You are setting off on a very important job, and I should like you to know that I have been assured that no better, fitter and braver men could have been selected than you to play this very vital role.

"You have been specially trained for a job like this and provided with every piece of equipment you should require. I know that you will tackle this job with determination and enthusiasm, and with a bit of luck I am sure you will pull it off. We shall be waiting to hear how you have gone on, waiting to learn what British paratroopers can do."

The tone of his voice changed and lowered: "I decided that I just couldn't let you go without coming here to say goodbye to you." Some of the men experienced a strange feeling. They were acutely aware that he had not said "Farewell". He had said "Goodbye". Was the word prophetic? But no sooner had the thought materialized than the men dismissed the idea. It did not do for soldiers to think too deeply about the precise meaning of such words.

The admiral's voice lowered still further, almost to a whisper. "A pity," he said softly. "A damned pity." He was not speaking to them. It was a private thought escaping as a mere murmur.

Only the trooper standing nearest to him caught the words. For some time afterwards he considered them, trying to infuse a meaning. After a great deal of thought, which brought no effective result, he mentioned what he had overheard to his comrades. Later they were to realize what possibilities had occurred to the admiral.

But at the time the moment passed quickly. Admiral Keyes resumed his normal, confident voice. "We are very proud of you," he said. Then he drew himself to attention, erect and impressive in his uniform.

And *he* saluted *them*.

The men were taken unaware by this sincere and unusual gesture. It was like a moment out of time and out of place. *They* returned *his* salute, their arms going up in ones and twos until finally, scarcely able to believe their ears, the whole parade was stiffly at the salute.

The admiral knew just what the troop were being asked to do. He knew they were guinea-pigs, and at this final zero hour he was not a little overcome. Obviously a man capable of emotion, he turned abruptly and walked away.

At dusk the eight Whitleys took off for Malta. Lieutenant-Colonel Rock and Wing Commander Sir Nigel Norman went with them, the former to remain for a few days afterwards in Malta and the latter to fly on in one of the two aircraft scheduled to bomb Foggia, thereby to witness from the air the descent of the paratroopers on the Tragino aqueduct before returning to Malta. What the raid was to mean for the thirty-five paratroopers was well appreciated, and neither Rock nor Norman was expendable. They were considered too valuable to the parachute school to be exposed to that sort of danger.

The commando made a direct flight across enemy-occupied France, the men experiencing from time to time the flash of anti-aircraft guns attempting to shoot them down and the flak rising up towards them like orange-coloured snowballs in the night. None of the aircraft was hit, and they counted themselves lucky that the flight as a whole was not attacked by German night fighters. Only one of the planes, flying at some distance from the others, was sighted by a German fighter, which chased it for a time. The Whitley pilot took evasive action and was eventually fortunate enough to shake the offending craft off before it was close enough to use its guns.

At dawn on 8th February they were over Malta, circling and talking to ground. "You cannot land for at least an hour," the pilots were told. "There was a bombing raid by the Germans during the night, and the runway is in a pretty poor condition. We're filling some holes in for you to land." Later all eight Whitleys landed safely.

Operation Colossus could not begin at once. Bad weather had prevented a new set of photographs being taken of the target area, and it was decided to wait until this could be done. The next day Flying Officer A. Warburton DSO, DFC, a famous member of the Photographic Reconaissance Unit, flew over in a Glen Martin and secured some excellent pictures. These showed not one but two aqueducts spanning the Tragino south-west of Monte Vulture. They were two hundred yards apart, one larger than the other and clearly defined amid the snow-covered mountains. The larger one was singled out for attack.

Now they waited for one thing – a suitable weather forecast. Maps were issued to the officers and the plans gone through many times.

"A dry cold, night with moonlight over southern Italy." That was the weather forecast for the next evening. The next evening it was.

During the day there was something that could not be forecast – raids by enemy bombers.

Containers with explosives, rifles, sub-machine guns and bren-guns, all attached to parachutes, were being loaded into the racks where the Whitleys normally carried bombs. Lance-Corporal Jones was supervising this work, carried out by a squad of Maltese workmen. At the first wail of the air siren the workmen laid down their burdens and began to run for shelter.

"Come back," shouted Jones.

The men halted and turned, looking at the corporal sullenly and making no attempt to obey.

"Come back and get on with the job," yelled Jones.

"No, sir," returned their spokesman. "You say those things explosive. You say handle them careful. It will be pretty damn dangerous if we do job during air raid."

"It'll be pretty damn dangerous if you don't," bawled Jones, drawing his .32 Colt automatic and pointing it at the speaker. "Because if you don't get cracking and get this aboard, I'll shoot you. And that'll be even more dangerous. Understand?"

"Understand, sir," came the reply.

The loading was completed, with Jones's pistol in his hand. "I'd have used a shot or two," he said later. "First as a warning, then for real."

The men drew rations — slabs of pemmican, hard-tack biscuits, chocolate and raisins — designed to last them for six days. Their water bottles were filled, and each man was given a cigarette supply. These were stowed in haversacks, billy cans and pockets, the haversack of one man in five being reserved for carrying a small stove which worked with a solid fuel and was smokeless. Each man carried a box of matches. Each of those troopers who had been in the Royal Engineers before volunteering for the commando carried a tin containing cotton wool and a dozen detonators in a breast pocket, not the pleasantest thing to have on one's person in action or drifting slowly down through moonlight into enemy territory.

The trouser pockets of their battledress were lined with chamois leather so that each man could carry three hand-grenades. In web holster they had pistols, the officers .38 revolvers and the men .32 Colt automatics with four spare magazines. The commando knife strapped to one leg completed their personal armoury. Trooper Nastri, alias Tristan, carried a set of handcuffs, but for what possible use these were designed no one ever discovered. They wore fur-lined leather hats resembling flying-helmets, woollen gloves and new boots with thick rubber soles.

At 4 p.m. they were paraded for inspection by the Governor of Malta, General Dobbie. Another brass hat taking a curious look at them, they thought.

"We're a ruddy peepshow," grumbled one trooper. "We might as well be in a cage."

"For generals, for looking at, for the use of," quipped another.

"Well, what did Admiral Keyes say at Mildenhall?" a third trooper suggested. "He said he was waiting to see what British paratroopers could do. Isn't it obvious? We're doing something no other British soldiers have done up to now. That's why they all come to see us, just as though we're monkeys at a zoo."

At 5 p.m. the troop were given hard-boiled eggs and hot, sweet tea. No one felt hungry.

As the evening shadows lengthened over the hangars, the runway and the waiting Whitleys, Major Pritchard gathered them all together and made his speech. It had a bearing on their talk about brass hats coming to look at them, for it was his speech dubbing them, in as many words, 'guinea-pigs' – a famous and well-remembered speech it turned out to be because of what was to happen to 'X' troop.

"Only now can I let you into the big secret of this trip," he also told them. "The job on which you are now embarking is an experiment to see what you can do. We are to jump right into the middle of Mussolini's Italy and blow up a big aqueduct which takes water to a large military area.

"After we have accomplished that job – and we shall see to it that we do – the only way out will be across mountainous country, but we will come to that obstacle when our job has been done."

He grinned and added: "Quite simple and straightforward, and I should like to wish you all the best of luck."

He did not tell them about the promise he had been given of assistance to get them out of Italy and away from the clutches of Mussolini's countrymen, who would be enraged by the raid, especially if it were successful. Perhaps he could not quite see the rescue plan coming off, and in any case there were those bitter mountains to traverse before they could even look for the friendly hand reaching out towards them.

CHAPTER EIGHT

A submarine to stand by

Major Pritchard had said nothing to the men about the official rescue plan. Bold in conception, dramatic, not unlike an episode in a thriller, it was also problematical. He did tell his officers before they boarded the planes on the evening of 10th February.

"After we've knocked that aqueduct for six," he explained, "all we have to do is get out of Italy. Don't tell me that's going to be a trifle difficult. I know it is. Don't tell me it can't be done. We're expected to do it.

"We're making for the mouth of the River Sele – it's shown plainly on your maps – here. Don't bother to assess the distance. It's all of sixty miles.

"Now we may get separated on that journey. Anything could happen after the big bang. So you've got to know what to look for when you get there. A British submarine, gentlemen.

"My information is that the sub *Triumph* is already standing off the mouth of the Sele. It will be waiting for *us*. We're supposed to get there by the night of the 15th-16th. That gives us say five days to get there in time. The sub is to rise to the surface on that night and send a flash signal periodically."

To the major and his officers, pocketing their maps, the possibilities or probabilities of the submarine being at its planned station, whether they could make the rendezvous in five days and *if* they could get there, were imponderables which they did not bother to discuss.

"To change to another subject, gentlemen, I'd like to check on something. You know what to tell the men during the flight about the drill for assembling in darkness after the drop?"

The five officers assured their CO that they knew what to tell the men.

"OK," said the major. "Off we go then."

The men boarded their planes laughing, joking and singing. An observer might have imagined they were soldiers being flown home on leave.

Colonel Rock was one of those who stood on the tarmac watching them go. He was to return to Ringway and write a report for the War Office on the training of the paratroopers, the organization of the mission, and the morale of the men. Included in that report was this: "When the men left Malta, their morale was terrific. A more cheerful and born leader than Major Pritchard could not have been found anywhere."

When the eight Whitleys lifted off the runway, gained height slowly and in the gathering dusk turned away from Malta over the sea, there were still about four hours to deadline. Waiting is never easy, specially for soldiers going into action, and that was a long time to wait. Colonel Rock knew this when he noted that, in spite of the time that must elapse before they jumped, the men were so cheerful. He likened them to excited youngsters unable to wait before setting off on a picnic.

But there was a reason for the early start. Night raids on Malta had become frequent, and the little air armada had to be in the sky before the first Nazi bomber throbbed overhead. The flight distance to the target was comparatively short, across the tip of Sicily and on over the toe of Italy. But once in the air there was time to spare, and the Whitleys took wide sweeps across the sea using it up.

The paratroopers made themselves as comfortable as possible in the dimly lit bellies of the planes. In some aircraft they sang song after song, including their *pièce de résistance*, new words written to an old tune by one of the men before embarkation. *Their* refrain began. "Oh, What a surprise for the Duce!" *They* did not give a moment's thought to an old superstition that it may be unwise to make foregone conclusions.

Lieutenant Deane-Drummond made a suggestion to the five men in his plane. He pointed to a number of inflatable mattresses stacked aft. "Why not use those to lie on?" he said. "There's a lot of time to kill, and you could all have a good sleep. Do you a power of good." He remained awake, wearing the inter-com earphones which kept him in touch with the pilot and listening to the men snoring peacefully. That was after he had given them the instructions Pritchard had laid down for assembly after dropping.

"We hope to jump in bright moonlight," he informed them. "I know it sounds damn risky – the Itis might try shooting us up before we're down, or mark the spot where we land and come after us. But the pilots can see better to drop us right on target, and once we're down we can see better to do our job. Unfortunately we can't have it both ways, but that's life isn't it?

"Despite the moonlight, however, it'll be dark enough to make recognition difficult. So we've decided on a drill using certain passwords. If you see a figure in the dark while we're mustering on the ground, you are to shout, 'Heil Hitler'. If the reply is 'Viva Duce', you'll know all is well. If not, it'll be an Iti, and you are to shoot to kill."

In the dim light they could see a grin on the officer's face as he added quickly: "And if you forget the 'Viva Duce' bit, for God's sake shout, 'It's me, Bill,' or something – or you won't shout anything else again.

"Now what is the challenge?"

"Heil Hitler."

"And the reply?"

"Viva duce."

"OK. Don't forget it. Now the moment each man lands, he is to search for our arms, ammo and explosives. They'll come down with us on parachutes. Try to mark where the canisters land and secure them quickly. OK?"

"OK, sir."

In the other planes the officers were also explaining the landing drill.

The Whitleys flew on. The pilots saw the coast of Italy ahead very clearly, the surf on the shores white in the moonlight.

At their first attempt to cross the coast they were met with an intense anti-aircraft barrage. They changed course several times before they could pass safely over into Italian air space. The distant thuds of the guns were muffled by the noise of their own engines and the walls of the fuselage, so the soldiers in the aircraft knew little of this – fortunately, no doubt, as they had enough to worry about under their singing and joking.

One of the paratroopers was not aware of any personal concern during the flight until he began to feel cold in the seat of his trousers. Fear, it was said, could affect the bowels to an unfortunate extent. Christ, he could not be as scared as that! He waited until no eyes were upon him. Carefully he slid his hand under his buttocks and was delighted to discover that all was well. There was a small hole where he was sitting and a cold draught of air striking into his seat. His only real fear had been that, if he had wet himself, what would the other chaps think? He was so relieved that he "almost enjoyed the remainder of the flight".

In Deane-Drummond's plane Sergeant Lawley was to be the despatcher, sending the other five out in quick succession and then jumping himself. Despite the lieutenant's comments on landing in bright moonlight, he, like the others in the aircraft, slept soundly.

In some of the planes the men had asked permission of their officers to open the trap door before the stand-by order came − "just for a look, sir". In the clear, cold winter night they looked down on the mountains of Calabria. The snow on the peaks glittered and shone in the moonlight, and they looked like gigantic cakes iced in white. It was a beautiful scene, but not the pleasantest one into which to jump, for there were many jagged peaks and deep ravines, and no doubt beneath the snow and mud lay hidden perils. A man would have to be completely unimaginative not to want an answer to questions like: Will I land in a ravine, a gorge or a river? Or come down on a steep mountainside? Will the aqueduct be heavily guarded? Could the enemy spy system have got wind of the operation, despite the strict secrecy under which it has been planned? But to all outward appearances the men were passing over such questions lightly.

Daly's was the plane with one man short. That meant four other ranks, just the right number for a game of cards. They played under the scant interior lighting of the aircraft.

In another Whitley, 'Big Jock' (Walker) interspersed the singing of their new theme song with a few Scottish folk numbers. 'Little Jock' (Durie) and 'Mad Bob' (Watson) told innumerable jokes. 'Flash' Henderson used his electric torch to read a book.

In one plane newly married Corporal Jones, the only man who knew when he volunteered that his duties would involve parachuting,

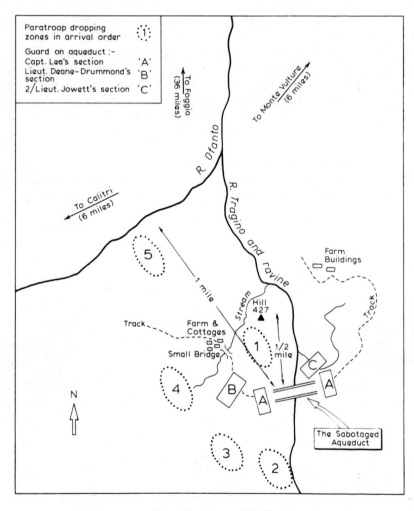

The sabotage area (detail)

read a book of poems with themes ranging from love to war and death. The anthology, edited by Herbert Read and appropriately entitled *The Knapsack*, was always kept in his kit. A line in one poem, he thought, was particularly appropriate to the moment. It read: "He was to sail down from the clouds."

Deane-Drummond's plane came in. When he got the pilot's fifteen-minute warning, he looked at his watch. It was 9.37.

The pilots were scheduled to begin the drop at 9.30 p.m., come in on their run up over the village of Calitri, descend to 400 feet over the River Ofanto and aim to drop the soldiers at map reference Hill 427. It had been a flight of well over three hours. The pilot had had to use up time because of the early start and make several detours to miss the worst of the Italian anti-aircraft fire. Seven minutes late. It was good flying.

Deane-Drummond handed the intercom helmet to Sergeant Lawley, who was to be despatcher and last out. The exit hatch was pulled away. The men clipped the static lines of their parachutes to the anchor bar. Deane-Drummond stole a penetrating glance at each of his men, produced a wide grin and did the thumbs-up sign. There were fifteen minutes to wait. It was a long time. Not a word was spoken.

With the hatch up, an icy draught blew into the plane. The howl of the wind outside the plane was like a Force 8 gale. In their battledress, jumping-jacket smocks, fur-lined helmets and gloves, they shivered. Outside the conditions must be Arctic. The plane droned on. A white world slid below. The lights of a town or a village appeared. Then a river gleamed in the moonlight beneath them. The mountains were desolate, wild, awesome, evil-looking. At the base of one of them a vehicle toiled along a lonely road. It looked like a bus. Or a troop lorry.

The first man sat on the edge of the hole, his legs dangling, his feet in what felt like an ice box.

The RAF rear gunner burst through from the tail end. "The pilot can't get you," he yelled. "The intercom must have failed at your end."

"What does the pilot want to say?" shouted Deane-Drummond.

"That you're due to drop in less than a minute. So get cracking."

Lawley remained standing. The others sat round the hole.

The green light flicked on. Where the hell was the red warning light? It should have come on first. That must have failed too.

"One," bawled Lawley over the engine noise and the wind. Out went number one.

"Two, three." Almost simultaneously went two more.

"Containers," shouted Lawley, pressing the button to release them. He waited seconds for the containers to go. "Four, five."

Lawley remained. He had no time to sit down on the edge of the hole. He whipped off the intercom helmet and stepped into it.

It was 9.42. The last man was out of that plane – only twelve minutes late.

Captain Daly's plane, a little late, was approaching the area, and if there can be such a thing as a voodoo, then he was certainly a victim of it. His was the aircraft from which a sick trooper had had to leave at Malta, and he was one man short.

Even before that, his plane had been delayed arriving at Malta from England by having to throw a Messerschmitt 109 off its tail. Only in his aircraft the rear gunner had been in action several times. Then, flying to Malta in bad weather, the pilot missed the base, had to take a fresh bearing and arrived eventually over the airfield from a different direction. His fellow officers who had then already landed at Malta, knowing that the flight was about the limit of a Whitley's range, had begun to say to each other: "Poor old Gerry."

Now Captain Daly was looking anxiously at his watch. Full three quarters of an hour earlier the pilot should have given him the stand-by warning. Long ago the red and green lights should have come on.

The pilot was in fact slightly off course, and Daly's worst fears were confirmed. He tried to talk to the pilot, who apparently could not hear him. Powerless to intervene, he heard the pilot and a member of the air crew talking.

"This doesn't look a bit like the target area," the pilot was saying.

"You're dead right, skip," came the reply.

"Looks more like the Adriatic than the Tragino place."

"Certainly does, skip."

"Strange really. It *should* be about here."

Daly felt the plane change course, banking steeply and turning. The pilot was going back the way he had come.

"We'll have another look further back," said the pilot.

"Wizzo, here it is." A voice crackled through on the intercom.

"This is the valley."

Then the voice addressed him: "Sorry we're a bit late, Captain, but here we are. You'll have to hustle a bit. Only a couple of minutes to dropping-time, I'm afraid."

Daly spoke into the mounting silence.. There was definitely something wrong with the intercom, and the pilot was unaware of it.

They opened the hatch. It did not look *just* like what he expected from the maps and models he had seen. What was more, there was no sign of the others having landed. Nothing was moving below. If they were on time, the first stick must have dropped almost an hour before. If they had dropped, what had happened to them? Perhaps they had been forced to lie low. Maybe that was the answer ... The red light went on. It flicked to green. Daly was acting as despatcher. He sent all four of his men out and pressed the button to release the containers. Nothing happened. He tried again. No joy. He jumped.

Daly and his men were indeed floating down into the wrong valley. Many miles and a great mountain separated them from the aqueduct and their comrades. It meant that the senior engineer officer, the man who was to mastermind the blowing of the aqueduct, would not be there to go into action.

CHAPTER NINE

Dropping in on the enemy

In one of the two aircraft that were to bomb Foggia, Wing Commander Sir Nigel Norman had a 'ringside' seat to watch the descent of 'X' troop at Tragino. All he had time to see were parachutes floating down in the moonlight. He was unaware that at least one plane was off course and that the chief engineer had been dropped in the wrong valley, where his skills could not be used.

He returned to Ringway in high spirits and wrote:

The night of the show was one of the most beautiful you can imagine, a full moon and glorious stars above patches of white cloud, the sea clear of mist and the snow-capped ridges of the Apennines glittering.

We could recognise every feature and landmarks as we came in, looking just like the landscape model we had used in planning the job and training the air crews.

It was easy to see the parachutes floating down. It was a moment one will never forget, but even more shall I remember the efficiency and the wonderful spirit of the men we dropped, their bearing, and the way they got into the aircraft at the take-off, singing a song, with special words of their own not particularly suited to the B.B.C.

The men employed on this task were specially selected and trained, carried very special equipment and were led by magnificent officers. The R.A.F. pilots who carried the force did their job with characteristic thoroughness and accuracy.

The flights were long, at night, a good deal over hostile territory and for long periods in bad weather, and the places they were navigating to were pinpoints. But they just ran to schedule.

But had he seen all the planes unloading? It all seemed very simple on paper. For the men of 'X' Troop it was not so simple.

The first man out of Deane-Drummond's plane actually landed at Hill 427, the pre-arranged spot about half a mile north of the aqueduct, just as though the air-crew of the Whitley had planted a bomb neatly on target. The whole plane load was in fact dropped in a very good 'pattern', all from 50 to 250 yards from the aqueduct.

Deane-Drummond himself was the fifth man out. Even before his parachute cracked open and jerked his shoulders, he was aware of a sudden great silence after the continual roar of the aircraft's engines. The first man out had not yet touched down. All four were descending below him. The containers, which had been released just before him, were not far away, swinging on their coloured parachutes. These had tiny, battery-operated lights on them to assist speedy recovery by the men. To any onlookers below, the canisters might seem like falling stars. At least that was what he hoped they would look like. He could see quite clearly below him the aqueduct spanning the Torrente del Tragino, a ravine filled with shrubs and small trees. Beyond it was a small hill and then the second aqueduct crossing a tributary of the Tragino, the Fosse della Cinestra. It was just like the air photographs and models he had seen. Only a damn sight wilder, more precipitous, the mountains an obvious hell to trek over. The trek, however, would come later. If all things were equal, that was.

At the moment he was rather busy. In fifteen seconds he would be down. He was anxious as to just where in this area of mountain, snow river and ice his feet looked like touching down. A bad spot could be disastrous. He did not like at all, for instance, the look of the country immediately surrounding the aqueduct. It was positively wild and perilously precipitous, much worse than they had been led to expect. Four hundred feet ... three hundred feet ... At about two hundred feet he saw clearly below him a small bridge near which a number of cottages nestled. And it looked to him likely, judging by his speed of descent and the angle of drift, that he would slap straight into it. If he did, he could knock himself out, break a leg, dangle from the bridge wall. He must prevent that. He pulled at the rigging lines of his parachute, trying to avoid the landing place which fate seemed to have chosen for him.

Thankfully he found himself drifting over the cottage roofs, over the bridge towards the gentle lower slopes of a mountain. Legs together, as he had been taught, soles of the feet as parallel to the ground as he could judge, he made ready to flex his ankles, knees and hips for the moment of impact. He did not like the slope, gentle though it might be. His feet touched. He pulled the rigging lines and rolled over. The canopy of his parachute settled over him, like a tent collapsing, and he could see nothing. But it was the most perfect landing he had ever made, better even than the best of his practice ones on flat, even grassland in Tatton Park.

His fist thumped the quick-release button on his chest. His parachute parted from him. He glanced down. The lower slopes of the mountain had been ploughed. Here there was no ice, only a sprinkling of snow, and the ground was soft. Jerking his head upwards he quickly took in his surroundings. He was only a hundred yards from the aqueduct. Was it well guarded? If so, he must have been seen. It was his first thought.

In the bright moonlight he scanned the countryside around him for the other five, who must already be down. No figure was to be seen. No shadow. Nothing moved. The intense silence characteristic of mountain country enveloped him. In the special circumstance of dropping in on enemy country, it was more than peaceful. It was eerie. His plane was to have been the third in. That there was no one to be seen forced him to realize that his aircraft must have been the first in. Something had gone wrong.

Not far from where he stood, the mountainside rose like a gigantic wall, part black, part snow-white, towering above him. At the foot of this giant, only fifty feet away from him, stood the bridge and the cluster of cottages. The lit windows seemed to eye him balefully. He shifted his gaze to the other side of the ravine. A track led from the farthest pier of the aqueduct, vanished over a hill and was seen again winding beside another group of buildings. It could be a farm and outbuildings. He knew that beyond the track, beyond two streams, lay a road which in turn led to a railway line and the River Ofanto. But for the ploughed land he could have been in a Scottish glen. It was peaceful and a little eerie.

Beyond twinkled the lights of Calitri, not far off. Its inhabitants were still awake. They must have heard plainly the throb of the low-flying Whitleys. They must, he was certain, have seen the parachutes descending in the bright night and landing as near as made no matter to the aqueduct. It was possible that the cottages so near to him housed a guard for the aqueduct. If so, how many did they number? And what was their weapon power?

Where were his comrades? And where in God's name was the nearest container with a stock of weapons? He scanned the mountainside, the ravine, the ground near the aqueduct, for the twinkle of a tiny light to guide him. He had only his revolver, and with the aqueduct so near to him he wanted a more serviceable weapon than that. Not one of the containers he had noted drifting down with him was to be seen.

After Sergeant Lawley, last man out, had 'walked' into the hole, he found himself floating steadily down into a twilight world containing the properties of fantasy. It was bright and bitter cold, and the snow-capped mountains on either side of him were bathed in a strange, luminous light. Worst of all was the silence. It was intense, unearthly. An impressionable man would have been completely unnerved.

He knew by the rate of descent that he would make a good landing. But that damned mountainside loomed even nearer. There was every chance, he thought, that he would land on an extremely steep slope. He would never forgive himself – and fate – if he were knocked out before the show started. In the event, however, he came down on a lower part of the slope than he had expected, not a steep part. For him too it was the best landing he had ever made. He crouched low as he punched at the button to release his parachute, listening in the infinite silence for the smallest sound. All he could hear was the drone of their plane receding into the distance. The noise of only one aircraft. Where were the others?

He drew his pistol and advanced stealthily in the direction of the aqueduct, which he had seen as he descended. After no more than twenty paces he halted. A dark shadow lay on the ground with a parachute trailing behind it. It was motionless. Was it one of his comrades, injured, even killed on landing? He ran forward, stooping, his feet sucked into the soft, muddy soil with each step. He breathed out hard with relief. It was one of the canisters, and the light on it was not working.

When he heard no other plane in the sky except the one from which he had jumped, and when he thought the inert canister was a comrade, a chilling fear had crossed his mind that he might be alone in this enemy wilderness. Now relief that it was not a colleague knocked out reinforced his doubts on the other question also. Quickly he opened the canister, grabbed a tommy-gun – and felt much better.

A figure loomed before him in the night.

"Heil Hitler!"

"Viva Duce!" It was Lieutenant Deane-Drummond's voice. "You OK, Sergeant?"

"Yes, sir."

"Good. I'll have one of those tommy-guns." The lieutenant helped himself from the canister, handled the gun lovingly and said: "That's a lot better, Lawley. So far, so good."

He was aware of a sound behind him, and he whipped round. A dark figure was bearing down the slope towards him, another was coming into view further back. Up came his tommy-gun. A third man was approaching from Lawley's side, and yet another behind him. But after a broadside of "Heil Hitlers" was rasped out and suitable replies received, all was well again. Deane-Drummond had all his five men around him.

"OK all of you?" he asked and received a reassuring chorus of affirmatives. "Any of you heard or seen any of the other Whitleys?" he asked then. None had. "Right," said Deane-Drummond. "See that building above the other side of the ravine? OK? It's probably a farm. But there could be guards there for the aqueduct. I want two of you to search the place." He detailed two men for the job.

"Now see those cottages near the little stone bridge? I want the rest of you" – he indicated the remaining three – "to do a similar job on those. Make sure you bring out every living soul. All of you take great care. If there are Italian soldiers there, and if they resist, use your weapons. We can't afford to lose a single man. I'm going to the aqueduct. Bring your prisoners to me there. And I repeat, take great care – I don't want any of you put out of action."

The two parties set off, and the lieutenant made his way warily towards the aqueduct. So far as he could see, it was deserted. There was complete silence. Standing near one of the piers, the cold made him cough. The noise was loud in the silence. If the Italians had a patrol guarding the aqueduct, he was bound to have been heard if not observed. But no voice came out of the night to challenge him.

"If there's no guard on the thing," he thought, "it might be a piece of cake." Later he added to himself: "If the others ever come."

If they did not, he was stymied. Neither he nor any one of his section was a volunteer to the commando from the Royal Engineers. They were strictly infantry. Not one of them had enough knowledge of explosives to blow up the aqueduct.

From the direction of Foggia he heard the dull and distant thump of bombs. No doubt the two Whitleys equipped for the diversionary bombing raid had got through and were at work. But where were the other five planes, those carrying the rest of the raiding party? Had they got lost? Were they in trouble? And were the six of them, in the new parlance of the day, on their own? Deane-Drummond cursed softly to himself.

He settled down, listening for a welcome drone. From time to time he scanned the sky. All he could see was the benign moon and the smallest drifts of cloud. Only the stars winked down at him. It was going to be a long wait ...

Sergeant Lawley and two men approached the buildings. They went slowly, treading quietly, crouching. A door opened, showing a momentary oblong of light, and a man came out followed by a dog. Lawley and the other flattened themselves. The man was whistling, the dog barking. Damn the animal! It might sense their presence and come nosing them out. The man disappeared into an outbuilding and a few minutes later re-entered the house with the dog, closing the door.

The three again advanced. At the door Lawley jabbed a finger at one of the troopers. "You stay outside. If someone comes out of the other houses, we don't want to get boxed up inside this one."

Lawley and the other trooper kicked the door open and entered quickly, their guns at the ready. They were in a stone-flagged, uncarpeted room of no great size. In the dim light of a paraffin lamp a middle-aged man, a younger one, a woman and several children stared wide-eyed at them from a plain wooden table. They were Italian peasants, and the shock of the sudden appearance of the commandos, obviously foreign soldiers to them, robbed them of speech.

"We have no wish to harm you," said Lawley. "Do as we say and you will be safe."

This was greeted by replies and queries in Italian, the words becoming more voluble by the second. Their speech meant nothing to the sergeant, who spoke no Italian and who was hampered by not having any of the three interpreters with him. He lowered the gun and took a step forward, holding out his hand to the more senior of the two men. Eventually the fellow realized that the soldier wished to shake hands, and as this was done, some of the fear drained from the man's eyes. Satisfied he had indicated that no one was going to be shot, Lawley pointed to them and motioned towards the door with his gun, whereupon they quickly donned warm clothes and allowed themselves to be shepherded outside. Lawley remained, searching every room in the house to make sure that no one was left inside.

With the family in the second house was an Italian soldier in uniform. In this house also the language barrier denied an exchange of understanding, and as Lawley stepped forward to shake hands with the elderly man, the Italian soldier made a dive for a shot-gun standing against the wall. Lawley beat him to the weapon and kicked it away, covering the soldier with his tommy-gun. "One more trick out of you, and I'll blow your guts out," shouted Lawley, "and if you don't understand our lingo, you'd better understand what this in my hands is for – and that I'll use it if I have to." The Italian understood.

When the cottages had been searched, the commandos turned their attention to the outhouses, which proved to contain no human life.

Altogether Lawley's party and the other two collected some two dozen Italians, men, women and children, all civilians except for the one soldier. They fell docilely into line and allowed themselves to be marched off towards the aqueduct, to a raucous accompaniment of barking from the dogs they had locked in outhouses.

All was so silent in the vicinity of the aqueduct that Lieutenant Deane-Drummond relaxed his wariness a little and sat down with his back resting against one of the piers, trying to wait as patiently as possible for the planes which did not come.

CHAPTER TEN

The saboteurs get to work

The other four aircraft had encountered ack-ack fire and sighted enemy fighters. They took evasive action, flying off course for a time. They were delayed. But at last they had the mountains of Calabria in sight. It was 10.15 p.m. and the pilots still had to find the correct approach and make their runs in to off-load their human cargo. It had been a long wait for Lieutenant Deane-Drummond.

Corporal Jones, the man who liked poetry, had just read a verse of a poem by Julian Grenfell several times when the officer in his plane received the early warning call from the pilot. The lines were:

And when the burning moment breaks,
And all things else are out of mind,
And only joy of battle takes
Him by the throat, and makes him blind.

"Fifteen minutes to dropping time." The commando officer repeated the pilot's words.

Corporal Jones thrust the book back in his haversack and helped to lift the trap door through which they were to jump. Sliding under them was a contour map of black and white desolation. Amid the towering peaks groups of lights winked.

"That'll be Calitri," said the officer. "We're on fifteen minutes standby. We'd better get prepared." Captain Lea passed on the message to his men in the aircraft, interrupting a discourse by 'Pop' Julian, a landscape gardener in civilian life, on how to build a garden wall. The words had the effect of bringing back to Julian's mind a jocular forecast made just before they left Ringway that the mission would result in a newspaper headline revealing: "Bridge Blown Up – Paras Not Heard of Since." He was soon too busy to think further about any imaginary newspaper epitaph.

In this plane it was decided that Sergeant Durie would be despatcher and Corporal Julian first out, followed by Trooper Ross.

"Don't forget the containers of arms and explosives will be released after half of our stick has gone out. You might spot them coming down alongside you. They'll have coloured parachutes whereas ours are white," said Lea. "Now check your static lines to make sure they're OK."

"OK, sir," they said.

The pilot of Second Lieutenant Paterson's plane gave the warning early. "Get yourselves ready, boys," said the lieutenant. "Twenty minutes to go."

Hunched against the fuselage wall, his six feet three inches cramping him in the small space, he was glad it was time to get out of the aircraft. He was called 'the big Canadian' to distinguish him from his countryman, 'Killer' Jowett.

He had decided to despatch the men himself and jump last, and he peered down through the hole when Corporal Jack Watson got the cover off. He saw the lower slope of a mountain with a patchwork of ploughed land beyond. Calitri lay below at a few hundred feet. The walls of the houses that caught the moonlight were pale, those in shadow black. A winding road girdled the mountain.

The red light flicked on, then the green. With a hand signal he sent the first, second and third tumbling out.

He pushed the button to release the containers. Nothing happened. He tried again. The containers had not gone. Rapidly he sent the other two men out. A few seconds delay could land a man a long way from the target area. He pressed the button again. Something must have jammed. He banged at it, but it was no use. "We're going in without our guns," he thought.

The engine note changed. The pilot was opening the throttle again. The plane was lifting to clear a rocky escarpment. He dragged off the inter-com equipment and jumped through the hole.

In another plane Sergeant Clements was to be the first to drop. He sat on the rim of the hole.

"Less than a minute and your jumping-light will go on," said the pilot through the intercom.

"Any minute now," said the despatcher.

Clements looked down on a river bed. The plane seemed to be following it. "God, not into a river," he thought.

The plane banked, turning off left, and the red light came on. Clements swung his legs into the hole. The green light clicked on momentarily, then reverted to red before he could launch himself. The aircraft began to rise steeply, and Clements saw rushing beneath him a granite escarpment. It was rocky, jagged, ugly. "That's even worse!" thought the sergeant.

On went the red light again – for ten seconds. Then the green – but it went on, off, on again. This time Clements launched himself forward, only to be grabbed and held by two of his comrades as the green light stayed out and was replaced by red, shining steadily. The plane circled to make a fresh approach. Clements could not have been in a more precarious position. One of his mates held grimly on to his jumping-jacket, the other clung to his parachute. He was half in and half out of the hole. It was impossible to drag him back. The small of his back was wedged against the rim of the exit, his feet dangling out of the hole. It took several minutes for the plane to come in on its run again. And all this time – an incredibly long time for him – Clements looked down on terrain in which it looked impossible for a parachutist to land safely.

At last there was a clear green signal and his comrades released him.

In two planes the containers jammed and failed to drop. In some the drop went like well-oiled clockwork. There was no hitch, for instance, in Pritchard's plane, the major jumping first, followed closely by Trooper Nastri. But in their case they and their equipment landed a long way from the aqueduct.

Below, Lieutenant Deane-Drummond was on his feet at the first distant drone in the sky. He strained his eyes in the direction from which he knew they must come, and at last he saw an aircraft, small in the distance. It grew in size and lost height, as it was supposed to do. And soon there was another following on ... and another ... His spirits rose like a speedometer needle when the foot jabs hard on the accelerator. He wanted to cheer. Everyone around him was looking upwards too, his five men, their peasant prisoners, the Italian soldier.

The planes came in one after the other, roaring low, and the parachutes, silver white in the moonlight, were a strangely beautiful sight, like droplets from the moon floating down peacefully upon the earth. It was a spectacle never before experienced by the Italian peasants. Or by much of the world for that matter, for a raid by paratroops was indeed something new. The Italian children jumped with excitement and clapped their hands. "*Angeli, angeli*," they shouted, while their parents gazed with awe and crossed themselves. No angels these, however, even though they were later to give part of their chocolate ration to the children.

Lance-Corporal Jones's parachute cracked open like a circus whip within two seconds of his leaving the aircraft. The slip-stream of the aircraft had hit him hard. Momentarily he was shocked, wondering if something had gone wrong. But he found himself floating nicely, and looking up he saw the canopy fully open and decided his parachute was safe. As he descended, the aqueduct, the mountains and the streams made a beautiful picture. All it needed, thought the poetry-lover, was a frame round it.

But for the intense cold, it would have been a pleasant enough descent. He found himself actually appreciating the stillness of the night. But he realized with a start that he was making straight for a ridge of trees. In seconds he would go slap into them. He pulled hard on his guidelines to clear them and, lifting his knees, missed the topmost branches by inches − only to land with a great splash in the middle of the Tragino River. If the canopy of his parachute had settled over him, he must surely drown. On his many practice jumps he had had some strange landings, including one into the middle of a midden. But he had had neither experience or instruction on what to do in a case like this.

He heaved himself to one side, falling full length, and found himself completely under water. Fortunately he came up not into a darkness that the canopy would have created but into moonlight. One end of the canopy rested wet on his shoulder. He had floated up only six inches on the right side. Mercifully, he was standing on the bed of the river. It could not therefore be so deep as he had feared. But the river was running swiftly, making wading difficult. He was in the predicament of an angler who might lose his balance while wading! By partly wading and partly crawling, with the sodden parachute a clinging weight on his shoulders, he at last made it to the bank and clung exhausted to a tree. Here he banged the release box on his chest and with infinite relief watched his parachute carried away swiftly on the current.

Hauling himself onto the bank, he coughed up and vomited the considerable water he had swallowed. He tried to think where the aqueduct lay, but the experience had clouded his sense of direction. The best thing to do, he decided, was to walk along the bank of the river in the hope of finding one or more of his comrades who still had to land or who had already done so. He knew he must keep walking to keep the blood circulating, for his drenched clothes must dry on him in the intensely cold night, and already the chill was numbing him.

He decided to proceed upstream, and as he walked he looked for containers. He had found none of them when from behind a bank he heard a hissing noise which he was at a loss to place, then a low muttering which was distinctly human.

From his pocket he took two grenades. Holding one in each hand, his fingers touching the pins, he looked over the bank. He opened his mouth to shout "Heil Hitler," but the words were not spoken. For a cheerful voice said: "Oh it's you, Doug. You all right? You look like a ruddy drowned rat."

Two of his comrades came round the bank and joined him.

"Which way to the aqueduct?" he asked.

"I make it this way," came the reply.

"That's the way I was going. I came down in the river, and it was a toss-up which way I should walk."

The three continued along the river bank and before reaching the aqueduct found and picked up two extending ladders that had been dropped by parachute and a four-foot-long canister containing four metal boxes.

Lance-Corporal Pexton sat on the edge of the jumping-hole and surveyed the scene below him. It was far from inviting. In the light of the moon the snow-capped mountains might have been floodlit. There were jagged ridges – like discarded sets of gigantic false teeth, he thought. There were steep slopes on which a parachutist would touch down at his peril. And there were points of blackness in the snow mantle that could be deep holes — holes out of which a man might never climb ...

A large vehicle moved slowly along a snaking mountain pass. Was it a troop carrier? Were the Italians preparing an unpleasant welcome?

"If I survive this lot," thought Pexton, "I'll admit to the other lads that I was plain stark mad to volunteer for anything as crazy as this." If he did survive, if he did make such a statement, it would be done in his characteristic joking manner. But even for a supreme optimist like Pexton the landscape sliding below the plane was an unpleasant sight and the thought of his impending descent into it not a little chilling.

He was out, falling, jerking, drifting. Assessing the line of his descent, he judged that there was a fair chance of his landing on even ground. But at the last moment there was an olive tree right in his path. He pulled at the guidelines but was unable to alter his line of descent.

The tree stood some fourteen feet high and, crashing into it, he dangled from its topmost branches. His fingers searched for his commando knife. He could not reach it. He tried to grip a branch to alter his position. It was beyond his reach.

The silence of the mountains enveloped him. The manner in which he hung afforded little vision of the surrounding countryside. His lips must be sealed. For all he knew, a shout might alert the enemy. At that moment he longed to hear a voice in the night accosting him with the words: "Heil Hitler." Whereupon he could answer: "Viva Duce — and damn well get me down from up here." With much wriggling, there was at last a branch he could reach. Twisting himself into a different position, one hand reached the hilt of his knife, and he set about cutting himself free.

His drop to the ground winded and jarred him more than any parachute landing had done, but he was uninjured and soon able to make his way towards the aqueduct. He came upon a group of figures in the darkness, but there was no need for him to shout the challenge for he heard this already being called and answered between them.

After his somewhat unorthodox exit from the plane, Sergeant Clements drifted to an ideal landing in a ploughed field, some eighty yards from the aqueduct.

Corporal Julian came down nicely and squarely on both feet on the pebbles of a dried-up stream, though narrowly missing both a clump of trees and a collection of large boulders at the side of a gully. There was complete quiet, no wind in the trees, no trickle of water on the dry pebbles. His pistol in one hand and a grenade in the other, he made cautious progress towards where he thought the aqueduct lay. He came across Lance-Corporal Watson, and together they moved on, overtaking Corporal Henderson, who was carrying a heavy bren-gun he had taken from a container he had found.

With so many rocks, ridges, steep mountainsides and ravines all around them, it was considered a minor miracle that almost all landed on good ground. In such terrain a large number of landing casualties was more than possible, and one man observed afterwards to his comrades: "Our prayers for happy landings have been answered."

In the event, only one man was put out of action, Lance-Corporal Harry Boulter, who on landing crashed onto large boulders at the side of the Tragino River. He broke an ankle and was out of the operation. Some of his comrades found him dragging himself painfully towards the aqueduct, helped him to a grassy slope and, following orders, left him to his own devices while the raid got under way.

As leader of the raid, Major Pritchard had wanted his feet to be first to clamp down on enemy territory, and it was a disappointment to him that his plane, scheduled to come in first, was in fact one of the last. And the more to upset his plans, it shed its load further away from the aqueduct than any of the others, setting them down almost a mile from it, near the River Ofanto.

Pritchard landed on pebbles at the side of the water, quickly released his parachute and took immediate stock of his surroundings. All was quiet, with no sign of an enemy presence in the immediate vicinity, which was initially at least a hopeful sign. But was that also the case at the aqueduct? What was occurring there in his absence? On his descent he had taken careful note of the aqueduct, which he could see comparatively plainly in the moonlight. He had seen groups of dark figures near to it. Were they all *his* men? Or was there an Italian presence at the aqueduct itself? And if so, what was the precise situation at this moment? He made no assumptions, did not allow his imagination to take over but concentrated calmly on gathering together the other five men who had jumped from his plane.

Nastri, his Cockney-Italian 'shadow', who had landed safely some twelve yards away, was the first to join him, emerging grinning from a clump of bushes. Within a few minutes the other four were 'all present and correct', having landed within a small radius of the commanding officer.

Pritchard had also taken careful note of the canisters descending from his plane and had a good idea where most of them had landed. These were therefore quickly retrieved and, armed with tommy-guns and carrying canister and other equipment, the major led the way in the direction of the aqueduct. He left only the forty-pound boxes of gun cotton, as taking these would have delayed his arrival at the aqueduct.

He and his party made steady progress, though they could not move as rapidly as he would have wished because it was necessary to traverse areas of mud from melting snow and climb at least one minor foothill.

As Second Lieutenant Paterson floated down, he saw below him to his right the canopies of five parachutes shimmering like huge, upturned, silver-grey saucers reflecting the bright moonlight. He too had seen figures around the aqueduct and wondered if his comrades from other planes were engaging the enemy.

His landing in fairly deep mud was soft, scarcely jarring his body, and he, like many of the others, was surprised at the silence when he had expected to descend to the rattle of machine-gun fire and the crack of rifles. There was no sound, except the distant barking of dogs. Unaware that these echoes came from the outbuildings of the farm raided by Deane-Drummond's men, the unwelcome thought struck him that his comrades who had dropped earlier had met a strong Italian presence and that possibly dogs were being used to flush out pockets of paratroopers unable to link up with the remainder of their force.

After a brisk climb with his five men, he reached the aqueduct, where he was relieved to find that most of the men from the first planes in had already assembled and that there was only one Italian soldier in evidence – and he a prisoner.

Major Pritchard arrived on the scene, and Lieutenant Deane-Drummond, who had been first to reach the aqueduct, reported to him that he had found the aqueduct to all intents and purposes unguarded and that he had rounded up all Italian civilians in the vicinity. He also passed on the news that Captain Daly, the senior engineer officer, was missing. It could only be assumed that his plane had either developed engine trouble or lost its way.

The major at once issued orders. The Italian prisoners were to be placed in one of the farm buildings at the other side of the Tragino. The sappers in the party were to scour the hillsides and farm fields to find and bring in the heavy explosives containers which had not yet been retrieved. The three infantry officers were to take up positions at all approaches to the aqueduct to guard against enemy interference while the preparations for the big explosion were taking place.

Lieutenant Deane-Drummond commanded the track leading to the farm buildings in which the Italians were locked. Captain Lea divided his party into two sections, placing one at the eastern end of the aqueduct and the other at the farther end of it over the Ginestra, while Second Lieutenant Jowett disposed his men downstream where the Ginestra flowed into the Tragino.

"At the moment we've got the aqueduct all to ourselves," said Major Pritchard. "That's a bonus we could hardly have expected, so we must take rapid advantage of it. But it's well on the cards we won't be left unmolested for long. It's too much to hope that not one of our parachutes was seen dropping, and enemy troops are probably racing here at this moment."

The only officer who had not yet received his orders was Paterson, but he was soon to hold a weighty responsibility.

The Major called to him. "Lieutenant Paterson."

"Sir."

"A word if you please. You're aware that Captain Daly isn't here?"

"Yes, sir."

"Goodness knows where he is, but he hasn't turned up. As junior engineer officer you were to be his assistant blowing this thing up. I'm afraid you'll have to mastermind the job yourself. OK?"

"OK, sir."

"Well, it's all yours, Paterson. In Daly's absence you know more than any of us about this job. Examine the aqueduct and decide how best to set about demolishing it. Handle it as you think best."

It was some time before the first of the heavy boxes containing explosives was manhandled to the aqueduct from the spot where it had landed. The major realized that this work must be completed more rapidly, not an easy task as some of the boxes, in particular those released from Pritchard's plane, had to be transported over fairly long distances.

He enquired how many male prisoners were locked in the farmhouse. "About a dozen or so," he was told.

"Right, get them out," said Pritchard. "Put them to work with the sappers."

The Italian men took their orders docilely and set to work, acting as porters for an operation designed to blow up their own aqueduct! When the interpreters put the order to them, they commented that they would be very willing to oblige, for nothing ever happened in this isolated area, and it would give them something to talk about for the rest of their lives. (It is somewhat amusing to consider that most of these Italian civilians were later awarded medals for their "gallant behaviour in the face of the enemy".)

Major Pritchard, a sub-machine gun across his knees, sat down with his back to one of the piers of the aqueduct, calmly watching the parties of workers toiling up the slope towards him carrying the heavy boxes, showing no outward sign of his impatience at the length of time the operation was taking. He noted that the sappers joked good-humouredly while the Italians were obviously grumbling and cursing in their own language, the hard work quickly undermining their original genial acceptance of the task.

The only other sound in the night air was the barking of the dogs. Pritchard was not too keen on the row they were making. He looked in the direction of Calitri and wondered if the inhabitants were sending messages afield to the effect that something rum was going on in the Tragino Gorge area.

From the direction of the village there came eventually a lone figure on a bicycle, pedalling down the track at the Ginestra side. Was some brave fellow coming alone to investigate? Deane-Drummond pounced on him and took him in charge. He turned out to be the local station master, and when he realized that he was a prisoner of British soldiers and that he was likely to be held for some time, he excitedly spelled out his main worry – that he might lose his job for being absent from his station. Repressing a smile, the lieutenant assumed an expression of the utmost gravity and said to an interpreter: "Tell him I will write a note for him explaining the reason for his absence." The station master, taking this promise as a solution to all his problems, smiled happily and allowed himself to be cajoled into helping his fellow Italians to carry the boxes.

The officers in charge of guarding the aqueduct told their men that, although they were thus far unhindered in their task, it was possible that a party of *carabinieri*, armed Italian police troops, would be in the habit of making regular visits to the aqueduct to make sure all was well. In the event of this happening, they were to try to take such a party prisoner in silence and only to fire if it were absolutely necessary. "We don't want to really waken Calitri up," they explained. "Not until the aqueduct's blown anyway. So keep your eyes peeled and listen for the slightest sound so that we might move into positions where we can ambush them – if they do come."

Meanwhile Lieutenant Paterson was making his survey of the aqueduct. It appeared to be much the same as the model he had studied at Ringway – with one vital difference: the centre pier was not at all low and squat as those models suggested. It was all of thirty feet high, and its feet rested in the centre of the water. It did not seem that pier, the most effective to blow, could be tackled at all.

That was not his only headache. They had been led to believe that the aqueduct was made of masonry, but ever since he had seen the latest photographs of it, brought in to Malta by Flying Officer Warburton, he had feared that the piers at least were made of sterner stuff. He took a chisel and hammer and broke the surface of one of the piers. It was reinforced concrete. It would take a great deal of blowing up.

CHAPTER ELEVEN

The big explosion

A grave-faced Paterson reported to Major Pritchard. "Afraid it doesn't look plain sailing," he said. "The aqueduct is one hell of a sight stronger than we thought. I'll do my best, sir ..."

"I'm sure you will, Paterson. We've come a long way not to have a go. What's your trouble?"

"Well, sir, Captain Daly's plan was to blow two piers and the abutment. That should have brought the whole thing down, specially if it had been constructed of less stern stuff. Most of the explosive we seem to have available has been brought in, and I reckon we might have six hundred pounds of gun cotton, seven hundred at the most, less than we'd counted on." (Two of the officers had already reported that their planes had failed to drop their canisters and boxes, and the load carried by Daly's plane could now be ruled out.)

"All right then," said Pritchard, "what do you propose to do?"

"The original plan will have to be ruled out, sir. I'm afraid I'll have to concentrate everything on one pier only. With a bit of luck that could bring the aqueduct down and pull the adjoining piers with it."

"Okay, carry on then," said Pritchard. "You're the expert now, and I'll stand by your judgement."

When almost all the boxes had been brought up to the aqueduct, there was further cause for alarm, a disturbing drone, distant and intermittent, breaking the silence of the pale night sky. That it was a plane was obvious, but, so far as they were aware, all their own aircraft had passed over, had long since turned for the flight back to Malta. Had the alarm been given? Had their position been pinpointed by the enemy? No man of 'X' Troop could deny the possibility that this was an Italian plane, fighter or bomber, homing onto them to strafe and bomb, to prevent the good work, at least to delay it while ground forces rushed to the scene.

The drone grew louder, and to its ominous sound was added the distinctive throb of a heavily loaded bomber. That it was making straight for their position was unmistakable. Soon it was flying directly over them. They strained their eyes to make out if it was a German, an Italian or one of theirs. It was almost above them, then it passed to one side of them and disappeared over a mountain top. It was believed afterwards that it was the Whitley carrying Daly and his sappers to the wrong valley.

There was, at all events, silence again, and hastily Paterson pushed on with his task. He chose the westernmost pier to receive their attentions and ordered the sappers to begin stacking the gun cotton against it. He was pleased about one thing. He now had a little more explosive than he had expected – 800 pounds of it. Of this he had 640 pounds placed against the abutment. Using ladders that had been dropped, Lance-Corporal Jones, Lance-Corporal Watson and others fixed a metal wire half way up the pier to facilitate stacking the explosives.

Suddenly they were aware that the barking of dogs had intensified. This was due to more howling from the direction of Calitri. If the dogs were alerted, then so were the little population. If not previously, then the nearby village must now know that there was something wrong in their vicinity. Its inhabitants must have been aware of the flight of the Whitleys, and someone surely must have seen the parachutes. It was impossible to believe that a village of the size of Calitri did not have at least a few telephones.

Paterson and the sappers produced the detonators from inside their shirts, where they had been strapped in tins containing a lining of cotton wool, not the most comforting items to possess on their drop from their planes. These were inserted in the explosive and the long fuses connnected. By this time an order had been sent down not to pass on any more explosive.

Deane-Drummond, stopping the last porter, allowed himself a rather satisfied smile. The track he was guarding passed over the Ginestra by means of the rough small bridge into which he had feared he might crash on his descent earlier. Constructed of concrete, it was just wide enough for a lorry to pass over it. He deduced that it had been used during the construction of the aqueduct and could be utilized again to bring troops to hinder their operation and for repair work or even reconstruction of the aqueduct. The lieutenant had already toyed with the idea that, if a little of the gun cotton were left over, it could be used to good effect on 'his' little bridge. He had been looking forward to having his own little private explosion, and now this seemed more than a possibility.

With help he got the wooden box in place just under one end of the bridge. Trooper Alan Ross placed a detonator in position and a fuse and stood ready to light it when the lieutenant signalled him to do so.

"Not a minute before I give the word," said the lieutenant. "Nothing must affect the big job." Officially Deane-Drummond was adding to the destruction. "Unofficially, I was blowing that bridge for the fun of the thing," he admitted afterwards.

Everything was ready for the big bang. It was fifteen minutes past midnight.

The Italians who had been helping to cart the boxes were taken back to their farm buildings. The sappers who had been assisting Paterson were sent back to join the rest of the party some distance from the aqueduct.

"When a single slab of gun cotton is fired, that will be the signal that the main charge will be blown one minute later." Major Pritchard indicated a spur of land about four hundred feet away. "So get yourselves tucked in behind that."

Pritchard exploded the small slab. His watch had a luminous dial. It showed the time at 12.29 a.m.

"OK then," said the major.

"OK," said the lieutenant, "and when we've ignited it, we've got sixty seconds."

Paterson and Pritchard lit the fuse for the main charge and ran for cover. They made for an outcrop of rock and threw themselves down behind it.

They waited. A minute, two minutes must have passed, they told each other. And no explosion.

"I wish we'd thought of counting up to sixty," said Pritchard.

Paterson began to rise. "I'd better go back and see what's gone wrong," he said. "It may be a faulty fuse."

"A moment," said Pritchard. "I'm coming with you."

They went carefully, treading lightly, as though they feared that a heavy footfall would set the explosive off. They had covered no more than a dozen yards on their way towards the pile of explosives when there was an ear-splitting crack and they hurled themselves flat on the ground and covered their heads with their hands.

A series of enormous explosions shattered the silence, as though each bang detonated another. They joined into one great rumble, a roll of thunder such as none had ever before heard, that echoed on and away down the valley of the Tragino. Flashes like bursting artillery shells lit the scene.

The men began to raise their heads above the spur behind which they had sheltered. It was a fantastic, flashing sight of dust and flame rising out of chaos. They saw in the foreground Pritchard and Paterson picking themselves up from the ground and running towards the aqueduct to inspect what damage had been effected.

The major and lieutenant halted some ten paces from where the explosives had been stacked – and what they saw made them momentarily inarticulate with excitement. Half the aqueduct was down. One pier had gone altogether. Another leaned at a crazy angle. Huge breaches cut gaping wounds into the concrete water runway. From these water cascaded into the Tragino valley. It poured from both the northern end, from which the water flowed, and from the southern end, where it flowed back to form a torrent spilling downwards, a spectacular, breathtaking waterfall, gushing into the ravine and flowing back into the valley beyond. It was a sight at which they wanted to gaze for a long time. But Pritchard said: "Come, we've no time to lose."

They took their eyes away from the spectacle and looked at each other. Neither spoke. Then they hurried back to join the others. They came up with huge grins shining through their dirty faces and their eyes sparkling. These told their own story, but they were assailed from all sides by questions designed to elicit just how successful the explosion had been.

Pritchard raised a hand for silence. "Listen to the sound of that water," he said. His words told it all.

For a moment the men stood in silence. The rumblings and the falling concrete were stilled, but the sound of falling water, huge amounts of it, was constant – and increasing in sound and volume. Then the band of men gave vent to their feelings. They had undergone a great deal of pioneering work back in Britain and come a long way to take part in this spectacular act of sabotage. Cheer upon cheer echoed across the valley, and Pritchard allowed them their enthusiastic demonstration. It was noise, but if the explosion had not raised the alarm and revealed their presence, nothing else would.

Deane-Drummond blew his little bridge while the explosions under the aqueduct were still reverberating. It was not identifiable as a separate explosion, but it afforded additional satisfaction for him and his section. They had made a good job of it. The explosion had cut the bridge neatly into two main pieces, which lay in the bed of the stream.

Deane-Drummond realized suddenly how near to the farmhouse his bridge had been. He and Trooper Ross came out of cover and ran to the building to see if any damage had been done to it or its inhabitants. One woman with a baby in her arms had run from the house, from which came wails of terror, though, as the two soldiers discovered, nothing worse had occurred than a quantity of debris raining on the roof. But the Italians were quite certain that there would soon be yet another explosion, in which their own building would go up – and them with it. That their children had been given chocolate by the raiders failed to dispel their fears.

In the event they were to be left quite safe by the "mad aliens from the sky", as the interpreters had heard themselves described. They were not even locked in. "You must stay inside these houses," they were told. "Most of us are leaving, but sentries are remaining behind outside, and if a single one of you steps outside, he will at once be shot dead." No such sentries were placed, but it is believed that the Italian peasants remained indoors for a considerable time.

As for the men of 'X' Troop, their mission was accomplished to the best of their ability. There remained the long trek, much of it over the mountains, through snow and mud, over desolate, open, enemy country where no help could be forthcoming – in a desperate bid to escape. It would take a long time, four days if they were lucky. And they were certain to be hunted all the way.

CHAPTER TWELVE

Goodbye to Corporal Boulter

The chances for the escape bid were not rated highly for the twenty-nine at the aqueduct, nor for the five dropped in the wrong valley. For one, Lance-Corporal Boulter, who had broken his ankle, they were nil.

He had sat in pain at the place to which they had carried him after his landing, his back propped against a boulder, and tried to watch the preparations being made by his comrades for demolishing the aqueduct. His disappointment at being unable to take part in this was intense, but when the explosion occurred and he heard the men cheering, he heaved himself slowly on to one foot and indulged in his own private shout of exultation. "Bloody marvellous," he said to himself over and over again.

He did not kick his ill fortune as such, resigning himself to the rule of the new commando unit, laid down from its inception and drummed into them all, that if a man had to fall out through injury or wounds, he was on his own, unable to expect help from those who had to push on. He had not yet given any thought to what his plans might be when the others moved out of the valley. There was, he thought grimly, plenty of time for that ...

The men assembled round their CO as he began to address them. "My thanks to you," said Major Pritchard. "You've done a splendid job. I'd just love to see old Mussolini's face when he learns of our raid and what we've accomplished. We must now withdraw — and lose no time about it. We've a long haul ahead of us, and the further we can get away from here before they come to see what's happened the better."

He paused, studying the faces around him, before continuing.

"We're deep in enemy territory and we have all of sixty miles to cover on foot before we reach the coast. I reckon we've a sporting chance of pulling it off, if we use the greatest caution and ingenuity and if we try to move forward only in the hours of darkness and rest up during daylight."

He then let them into the last secret of the operation. "There's something most of you don't know yet, and I'll tell you about it now. A British submarine has been ordered to rendezvous at the mouth of the River Sele, there to await our arrival on, it is hoped, the night of 15th-16th.

"If we push on hard, we should do it in time. It gives us four nights marching as from now. The plan is that the sub will take off in the dark and make for Malta, where with a bit of luck we should get transport back to England.

"But I'm not going to make light of the trip that lies ahead of us. It'll be a hard slog. Our route will lie across desolate and mountainous country, and in this winter weather I've no need to tell you it'll be damn cold. Much of our journey will be at two thousand and more above sea-level. What's more, the terrain is totally unknown to us.

"Within a few hours, possibly even now, our presence will be known, and the Itis aren't going to like what we've done. The whole country may be alerted, and certainly the part that lies between here and the sea. It is right that you should know the dangers that may lie ahead, and that the trip itself will be pretty hard going. But given just a spot of luck I believe we can do it. I reckon you're about the best trained bunch of chaps in the British Army at the moment, and I have every confidence in you."

Major Pritchard ordered them to dispose of the bren-guns and anything else too heavy to carry. It might be, he said, that they would need as many weapons as possible, but if they were to travel fast, they must travel light. "I'm afraid we can't have our cake and eat it," he grinned.

"By far the best plan is for us to split up into three parties. Smaller groups should have a better chance of getting through. Each party can take only one sub-machine gun and try to take a slightly different route while following fairly closely the main one. This has already been worked out by your officers, all of whom have good maps and compasses – not the ones in your collar studs, which are for a rather different kind of use and one we hope won't arise. The maps have been well studied, and I'm pretty sure we can maintain a good line towards the mouth of the Sele."

The officers in charge of each party were to keep as far as possible to the mountains, avoiding the roads, and, after making as much progress as possible each night, the men were to hole up during the day, doing their best to keep themselves completely hidden.

Second Lieutenant Jowett and Flight Lieutenant Lucky were to take one party, Captain Lea and Second Lieutenant Paterson another and Lieutenant Deane-Drummond and the major the third.

Pritchard raised an arm as though in a gesture of farewell to the two other parties. "There isn't much more to say except – good luck to you all."

The interpreters returned to the farmhouse to repeat the orders already given to the Italian prisoners. "We could tie you up with ropes and gag your mouths," they explained. "We could lock you in. But we're not going to make you uncomfortable. However, if you as much as poke a nose out of the door or window, it will mean instant death. We have sentries posted outside, and they have orders to shoot to kill at the slightest movement." As far as the interpreters could gather, the Italians believed every word, none of them realizing that every paratrooper would be moving off. Only the injured Boulter would know how long the Italians would remain indoors.

Major Pritchard had one more thing to do – say farewell to Lance-Corporal Boulter and do all he could for him before leaving him behind. He gave him a quantity of pain-killers, a compass and a map and told him about the submarine and where it would be waiting.

The major did not know if the ankle was broken or badly sprained, but he bound it up tightly with a damp cloth and strengthened it with a small splint. "Rest your ankle, Boulter. Take a pain-killer and another in about four hours, and if you feel up to it after a time, you might like to have a go at getting to that sub by yourself. Sorry we've got to leave you, but I know you understand the drill. I'm sure the worst that can happen to you is being taken prisoner and being out of the war. Keep your pecker up. And Boulter – good luck."

Pritchard forced himself to speak in a cheerful voice, omitting to show what he really believed – that, if it was doubtful that the others would reach the submarine, then there was no chance at all for Boulter.

"And by the way," added the major, "if the Italians do get their hands on you and chuck you in the bag, they'll be wanting to know a lot and asking a great deal of questions. It's understood that you can give them your rank, name and army number, and that's got to be their little lot. I know I don't need to tell you not to say how many of our chaps are here or where we're making for."

"I've not let you down yet, sir, and I'm not likely to now."

"Good man."

They shook hands.

"Good luck, Boulter."

"Good luck, sir."

Every man came to say goodbye to Boulter. Everyone knew what it was going to be like for him to be left alone. He knew too.

"On your way, you lot," he joked. "Don't waste time on me. I'm the lucky one. I've got out of that bloody long march over the mountains."

"It won't be all that long before we see each other again," said Lucky Pexton, aware that he was talking nonsense.

"You're dead right there, Lucky," said Boulter. "The time'll pass like a flash."

Every man handed him part of their chocolate and cigarette ration, insisting he took the gifts. "You'll have more time for this stuff than us," they said.

"What're you doing with those tommy-guns?" asked Boulter.

"Burying 'em," he was told.

"Well, for God's sake don't bury the lot. Leave one with me – and some spare ammo. Tag's a good 'un, the best there is, but he can't fool me. I might make it to the coast, he says. I'll become a POW. Well, I can think of one other possibility. When the Itis find me here, they'll be so bloody wild they just might shoot me out of hand. Now be good chums and leave one of those tommy-guns with me. If the Itis look like sending me to hell, I can then take as many as possible along with me. See?"

They left a tommy-gun with him.

The brens and most of the sub-machine guns were taken to pieces and pushed into the mud. Most of their weighty equipment was similarly disposed of. Each man kept his Colt automatic pistol and spare ammunition, commando knife, water bottle, mess tin and thirty-pound pack with food ration. Each of the three parties retained one sub-machine gun and several small primus stoves for making tea and boiling their ration of pemmican.

Corporal Henderson kept one of the brens out of reach of the 'burial party'.

"You know what Tag said," he was reminded. "It's too damn heavy to carry."

"I'll carry it somehow," said Henderson. "You never know, it might come in handy."

It was then about 1 a.m. on the morning of 11th February. The twenty-nine men were ready to move off.

Major Pritchard set off first. Without a word he began to walk in the direction of the foothills, and one by one his party fell in behind him, the mud on the slopes sucking at their feet. On went the major, setting a pace on firm ground which he was unable to maintain where soft earth and melting snow made the going harder.

They had not gone far when Deane-Drummond turned and ran back to Boulter. The lieutenant had already, with the others, said goodbye to the injured man and offered words of encouragement. Again Deane-Drummond shook hands with Boulter. There was nothing to say. It had all been said. They looked at each other, and then without a word Deane-Drummond hurried back to join his group, reaching them as they began the trudge up the first slope.

Soon all three groups were on the move. Boulter watched them all the way, mostly in single file, toiling up the slope of the nearest mountain, three long lines of figures in the moonlight. He saw them finally as small dark objects topping a distant shoulder of the mountain. One by one the distant figures reached the top and disappeared as they began a downward descent. Boulter watched until the last man had gone.

Some time later the pain became greater, and he discovered that it was due to swelling of the foot inside his boot. With his commando knife he cut away some of the leather and managed to haul the boot off. In place of it he wrapped his leather helmet round the foot and ankle, packed this with snow to try to ease the pain and tied the

leather on with string and a large handkerchief. Taking his haversack
and the tommy-gun, he limped off, slowly and painfully, in an attempt
to search his surroundings and find some sort of shelter from the
increasing coldness of the night.

Eventually he found a small wooden hut. It was empty, and inside
he lay down and dropped off to sleep.

As Captain Daly floated down after his four men, he became
convinced that this was not the valley of the Tragino. He had a clear
view of the terrain below him. There was no aqueduct to be seen, and
in the moonlight it should have been clearly visible.

In the whole valley there was not a house, not a farm building to be
seen. There was, however, one small wooden shed, and probably used
for sheep, and he realized he was making straight for it. Pulling on his
guidelines, he narrowly avoided it and made a good landing.

He looked around. According to the model and the photographs he
had studied, there were things he expected to see — trees, farm
buildings, the Tragino Gorge spanned by the aqueduct, a small bridge
over the Ginestra. There were none of these. The only things familiar
to the photographs and which he did see were mountains. And there
were plenty of those, all around him. It was mystifying until he studied
his map by the light of both moon and his torch. There he found the
answer. He decided that he and his men were in the next valley to the
one where they ought to be.

"You're not going to believe this, you chaps," he said as his four
men came up. "We've been dropped in the wrong damn valley."

Captain Daly knew that his plane was late. If the others were also
delayed, there might just be a chance he could reach them. But he did
not know that the others had been in the target zone for some time
and were getting down to work.

"We'd better try to reach the others," he said. "It's my job to blow
the aqueduct. Come on."

He started off up the slope, setting a good pace. He was in fact
leading the men in the right direction, but he was hopelessly short of
time. They were less than half way up their side of the mountain
when from beyond the ridge above them came the unmistakable
echoes of a big explosion. They halted and stood still, listening to the
rumbling dying away. Daly was forced to the conclusion that the job

had been done without his assistance. "Good man, Paterson," he said aloud.

Turning to the men, he said: "Judging by the sound of that explosion, the aqueduct has been blown to smithereens."

"What now then, sir?"

"It's pointless trying to link up with them now. By the time we got to the spot, they'd be well on their way along the escape route. They were to set off immediately the thing was blown, and no doubt all we'd find at the spot would be some very angry Italians. Our best plan is to make our way from this valley in the direction of the coast. Like the others, we must make our own escape."

"Pity we weren't in on it," said a disappointed voice.

"As long as the job's done – and I'm pretty certain it is – then that's all that matters," said the captain.

He then told his four men about the rendezvous that had been arranged with a submarine. He consulted his map again, led the way back down the mountainside and began to trudge westwards.

"Come on," he said. "We've got rather a long walk ahead of us."

CHAPTER THIRTEEN

A lone stand

The hut inside which Lance-Corporal Boulter took shelter consisted only of three wooden walls and a roof. It had no floor, only the rough ground, and was completely empty except for a small pile of straw in one corner. There were some wisps of wool clinging to the rough walls, and he guessed it was some sort of shelter for sheep or perhaps shepherds in bad weather.

He hobbled painfully into it, raked the straw to the middle at the rear of the hut, a point from which he would have a wider radius of vision, and lay down. His pemmican ration was useless, for he had no means of softening it with hot water, so there was no chance of a hot meal. But by the generosity of his comrades he had a plentiful supply of chocolate, nuts, raisins and cigarettes. He ate a fair amount of chocolate, took a swig from his water bottle and found himself yearning for a drink of tea – a luxury that in his case was impossible. After a time the pain in his ankle lessened a little, and he fell asleep with both hands on his tommy-gun – to wake shivering about half an hour after dawn.

He listened intently. The only sound was that of the water gushing from the broken back of aqueduct. He crawled to the front of the shack and looked out. The heights of Monte Vulture rose before him, dark, ominous and majestic against the pale glow of dawn. He looked downwards at the farmhouses. They appeared to be deserted. There was certainly no sign of life outside them. Boulter remembered being told: "You'll not have any trouble from the peasants down there. They've been told we've posted sentries who will shoot them if they come out." They won't stay indoors for ever though, he said to himself.

His throat was parched. He drank from his water bottle and decided that this must be replenished before anyone was astir. It was not yet full light, and he made his way, hobbling and resting, down to the water line. Filling his water bottle and drinking more, he made a painful ascent back to the hut.

An hour after full light, Boulter saw a door open at the farmhouse and a head thrust cautiously out. He assumed that with the daylight the 'prisoners' had looked out of windows and seen no sign of British soldiers. The head was withdrawn, and after a pause a figure stepped out and looked around. From his hide-out the corporal could just make out that the man was in uniform. He was obviously the Italian soldier assumed to be home on leave. He looked quickly both ways and ran to the outhouse. Apparently satisfied that it contained no alien commandos, he returned to the house. Several minutes passed and he came out again accompanied by two more men. The three went to another outhouse and appeared with a bicycle. The Italian soldier mounted it and rode off in the direction of Calitri.

Boulter directed a burst from his sub-machine gun in his direction, but the man was not without courage, for he pedalled on furiously on a track that led downwards and was soon out of range. "He's gone to raise the alarm," the corporal said to himself. "He'll probably be awarded a medal for heroism in the face of the enemy, or at least get a couple of stripes." The paratrooper then told himself somewhat ruefully that he had revealed his presence and his position. He began to drag himself further up the hillside. The pain he suffered was excruciating, and he gave up the struggle when he reached a boulder, behind which he wriggled. He feared he had broken a bone in his ankle.

Long before the soldier could have reached Calitri on his bicycle, two cars bounced up the rough track to the farmhouse. They contained two *carabinieri* and several civilians carrying shot-guns. They had been engaged in searching the countryside after the explosion had been heard in Calitri. From their position at the farmhouse they could see the shattered aqueduct and the water pouring from it. One of the cars left, the other remained, and one of the *carabinieri* made his way to the aqueduct, remained for a short time and returned to the farmhouse.

It was not until a truck arrived filled with Italian soldiers that they came up for Boulter. They made first for the shed, halting some distance from it and shouting. Receiving no reply, they fired their rifles at the shed, then rushed in. Finding no one inside, they fanned out in a semicircle and continued upwards in the general direction of Boulter's boulder. One *paracadutista* at least, they had been told, had been seen, crawling upwards from the shed.

It was obvious to Boulter that he would soon be seen, certainly if they moved beyond his piece of rock. He levelled his tommy-gun and fired. His assailants dropped to the ground and fired their rifles from a lying position. Then they crawled forward. Boulter fired again, and they retreated. He was a little disappointed with the tommy-gun, feeling that, if it had been a rifle, he could have picked them off one by one, even though they were some distance away and lying flat. He held them off until the magazine was empty, groped in his satchel for another clip and could not find one.

It was only a matter of time before the Italians realized he must have run out of ammunition. Then they surrounded him. A *carabiniere* sergeant handcuffed him, and a soldier tried to prod him to his feet. The pain in his ankle was now so great that he could not rise from his knees. There was a great deal of shouting in Italian, and he pointed to his ankle. But the Italians set about beating him up. They kicked, punched and clubbed him with rifle butts. His uniform was torn during this treatment, and a corner of one of the maps sewn into his tunic was revealed. This may have saved his life, because his captors turned their attention to the map, which they examined thoroughly. An officer pocketed it. Boulter was then hauled to his feet and made to hobble to Calitri, his captors prodding him on. Every time he stumbled and fell or limped too slowly for their liking, he was again belaboured with rifle butts.

At Calitri he was bundled into a car and taken to Naples Central Prison, where he kept repeating the words 'Red Cross' and pointing to his damaged ankle. Only then was a doctor called to attend to his injury. His ankle was in fact fractured.

The next day a long series of interrogations began, conducted by an Italian officer who spoke English. The main question, repeated again and again, was: "How many of you English descend at Tragino?"

"My name is Harry Boulter, I am a Lance-Corporal in the British Army, and if it's any good to you you can have my Army number."

"I will write that information down, Corporal. But I will ask my question – eternally if you understand – until you give me the answer good."

Stolidly Boulter gave the same reply, name, rank and number.

The second most important question in the officer's repertoire was: "You will tell me, pleece, where your comrades were going after they do much damage to the aqueduct."

"How the hell do I know? I wasn't with them. They had to leave me there with a gammy leg."

"Gammy? What you mean?"

"Injured."

"Ah, but you know good to where they were marching? They would have a plan, no?"

"The only plan I knew about was the one to blow your bloody aqueduct to smithereens."

"But your officer who commands, he would know where he wished to go, yes?"

"If he did, he didn't tell me. I'm only a bloody lance-corporal. But I don't think he had a *plan*, as you say. I think they just buggered off after the explosion."

"Buggered off?"

"Scarpered."

"Scarpered? Beware, soldier. I am not good and kind when I get annoyed."

"You don't speak English very well, do you? All right then – they just ran away, got the hell out of it."

"It is wrong words you speak, Corporal. Your commander would think what direction would offer best means of escape, eh?"

"If he did, he didn't tell me. I wasn't interested anyway. I was in great pain. And do you think he'd be fool enough to tell me so that you could get it out of me? Ask *him* when you catch him, *if* you can catch him. But he wouldn't tell you what time o' day it was."

"What is his name, pleece?"

"Ask *him* when – and if – you get him. He'll tell you his rank and number as well. But I don't think he'll tell you much else."

"How many of you *paracadutisti* drop into Tragino?"

"About fifty-five thousand."

"Do not be English comedian. You are insolent, and I like it not.

The number of your comrades, pleece?"

"You know as well as me that as a prisoner of war all I need to tell you is my name, rank and number – and not another bloody thing. That and the name of my CO are the only things I know out of all your questions. I'm not telling you those. The other questions I couldn't answer because I don't know the answers."

"I am persistent."

"I'll give you that."

"So – have other parties of English *paracadutisti* landed in other parts of Italy, or do they intend to?"

"God Almighty! Our top brass might know. If you think I could answer that one, you're off your rocker."

"Rocker?"

"Mad."

"It is you who are mad, Englishmen, you *paracadutisti*."

"I'll give you that," said Boulter, grinning through the pain of his ankle and the beating he had survived when caught. "God's truth, I'll give you that."

The interrogation went on for several days. Always they were the same questions. Always Boulter's answers were in similar vein. It was a great strain, particularly as he was not in good shape. But for one thing he was thankful. He was not tortured.

CHAPTER FOURTEEN

The Longest Night

Of the three parties making their way out of the Tragino valley, the one led by Major Pritchard and Lieutenant Deane-Drummond was the largest, a dozen men in all.

Making their way first through the muddy fields, they expected the tough going to tire their limbs, but they kept their eyes on the snowline above, where they were making for and where they expected to reach firmer ground. But when they began to climb the slopes, they encountered as much deep mud as on the flat fields below. They had to haul themselves up, digging into the slime with anything that came to hand – a commando knife, a sub-machine gun, a stick broken from a tree, sometimes clawing at the mud with their hands. Sometimes they made progress; sometimes they slithered back. It was agonizingly exhausting. It required all their will to make the ascent, aided to a degree by the high spirits which the success of the big explosion had engendered. In time, however, their cheerfulness was to be undermined by the exhaustion of the climb and the bitter coldness that, for all their effort of movement, penetrated through their clothing.

To add to their difficulties, there were steep gorges they had neither seen from below nor expected, some of them impossible to traverse. There were also snow-filled holes, some discernible because they were as large as quarries, other smaller ones that were not – and into which some of them fell and had to be hauled out by comrades linking arms to reach them.

Pritchard halted his men at roughly three-quarter-hour intervals, telling them to rest as best they could, then rising from the ground after a short pause and leading them on.

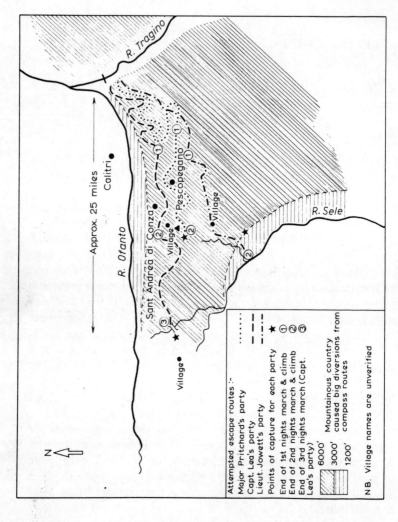

Escape routes and capture points

This old, cracked wartime photo of the members of 'X' Troop was taken just before they left Britain for the raid. On the front row, seated, from right to left: 1st, Corporal Pat O'Brien; 2nd, Lance-Corporal 'Flash' Henderson; 3rd, Second Lieutenant Jowett (with Scottish bonnet and moustache); 4th, Captain Daly (with hands to head adjusting jumping-helmet); and 7th from right, Flight Lieutenant Lucky (the broad man with his head tilted upwards). On the third row, Sergeant Joe Shutt is shown fourth from right; on the back row, the man at the far right is Trooper Alan Ross.

The aqueduct to be blown up by the paratroopers. This photograph was taken at the time of the aqueduct's construction and shows in the foreground huts used by the construction team which were not there at the time of the raid. But shown beyond the aqueduct are the farm buildings which *were* there and whose occupants were taken prisoner by the paratroopers.

Major T. A. G. Pritchard, CO of 'X' Troop, who led the raid. This photo of Major Pritchard (now Lieutenant-Colonel Pritchard-Gordon, DSO MBE) was taken in India before the Second World War.

Lieutenant (eventually Major-General) Anthony Deane-Drummond – a photograph taken later in the war when he had been promoted to major.

Captain (in this photo, c.1940, still Lieutenant) Christopher Lea. He was promoted major after his return to Britain from POW camp.

This photograph was taken at the POW camp at Sulmona, Italy, in 1941, by the Red Cross. It shows some of the men of 'X' Troop who took part in the raid and also six RAF and Army men in captivity with them. These six, unnamed here, are 3rd, 9th and 12th from left on the back row, 5th from left in the middle row, and 3rd and 4th from left in the bottom row (seated). Excluding those, the members of 'X' Troop are as follows. Back row, from left to right: 1st, Lance-Corporal J. Maher; 2nd, Sergeant J. Walker; 4th, Lance-Corporal D. Jones; 5th, Corporal P. Julian; 6th, Trooper G. Pryor; 7th, Trooper D. Struthers; 8th, Corporal H. Pexton;

10th, Corporal J. Grice; 11th, Sergeant A. Lawley; 13th, Lance-Corporal D. Henderson. Middle row; from left: 1st, Trooper R. Davidson; 2nd, Trooper J. Parker; 3rd, Lance-Corporal R. Watson; 4th, Trooper A. Ross; 6th, Sergeant E. Durie; 7th, Sergeant P. Clements; 8th, Trooper E. Samuels; 9th, Trooper D. Phillips; 10th, Trooper E. Humphreys. Bottom row, seated, from left: 1st, Sergeant J. Shutt; 2nd, Corporal P. O'Brien; 5th, Trooper Nastri; 6th, Corporal D. Fletcher; 7th, Trooper J. Parker.

Above left: Sergeant P. ('Clem') Clements. On his return to Britain he was promoted to full Lieutenant (when this photograph was taken) and continued war service in a parachute regiment.

Above right: Sergeant Arthur Lawley, shown here later in the war in his new rank of sergeant-major.

Trooper 'Nicky' Nastri.

Above left: Lance-Corporal Doug Jones, photographed at the time of his marriage, a few days before he left England on the raid.

Above right: Corporal Philip ('Pop') Julian, photographed while he was a POW in Italy.

Recent photographs of Lance-Corporal Harry Pexton (*right*, *above*) and Corporal D. Fletcher (*right*).

A photograph of 'X' Troop taken in 1942 when they had been sent from Sulmona to Campo di Lavoro 102. Top row, from left: Lance-Corporals Henderson, Pexton, Maher and Tomlin. Second row, from left: Lance-Corporal Watson, Troopers Phillips, Samuels, Humphreys and Pryor and Sergeant Durie. Third row, seated, from left: Trooper Parker, Sergeant Walker, Corporal Grice. Bottom row, from left: Corporal O'Brien, Trooper Nastri and Sapper Davidson.

"We're making some headway," he told the men. "But we'll have to get stuck in and keep at it. Anyone who can't keep up with the rest will have to fall behind or fall out, and any man who does that can't expect any help from the others. You know the rule that's been laid down in this troop. It's a golden rule for an operation like this, and it will be adhered to."

His plan was to climb to a ridge and then follow it, judging that this would keep them on a route to the Sele watershed. He hoped to traverse the north side of the Sele valley and make for the Mediterranean.

Many ravines they encountered, which had been impossible to detect from the valley below, proved to be impassable, and they had to use time they could ill afford to make detours. On the reverse slopes they could do little but allow themselves to slither down. But though less exhausting, this proved to be a dangerous business. There were deep fissures that by good fortune every man managed to avoid and hidden boulders into which they crashed from time to time.

It was a remarkable quirk of luck that on that first night's 'march' no one was injured or killed. It was the longest night any of the men in the three separate companies had ever experienced. And at the end of it Corporal Henderson still clutched his heavy bren-gun. How he had lugged it across such terrain, without a single grumble, no one could understand. That in itself, his comrades realized, was a minor miracle. As dawn began to light their surroundings, revealing the outlines of the snow-girt peaks more starkly than ever, Jones, who was carrying the magazine for him, suggested that he throw the gun away.

"Not bloody likely," said Henderson. "Italian troops are sure to be after us like ferrets, and they're bound to be in one hell of a rage. Apart from this bren we've only got one tommy-gun among the twelve of us. No, Jonesey, I'm determined to keep this bren — it can do a hell of a lot of damage."

That night highlighted the fact that fear assailed the men in different ways. All were courageous, but courage contains an element of fear, and human beings differ in the way apprehension affects them. Some had been unable to repress a secret dread of leaping from the planes into the unknown; others had scarcely given this a thought.

Lance-Corporal Jones, the man who had read poetry on the flight, for instance, the only one who had known it was parachuting he had been volunteering for, had not suffered a moment's anxiety about the jump into the Italian mountains. But there was a time when he knew fear on that Herculean upward fight to gain the ridge Pritchard was making for.

A landslide had occurred while they were scaling a steep upward slope. There were cracking sounds in the night, and a rumbling from above, increasing in intensity. A great mass of mud and snow and stones was dislodged from the mountainside above them. It began to slide like creeping, molten lava from a volcano. It would be impossible to avoid the stuff sweeping over them. Behind them yawned a sheer drop of two to three hundred feet, and the evil black mass looked as though it would take all before it. Including them.

Jones was one of those who was chilled with dread. Yet others who on the flight had been unable to still the fear of the forthcoming jump from the aircraft were able to curse and joke as they clung to the mountainside while the avalanche of mud, snow, boulders and rubble slid over and round their bodies and rattled echoing into the void behind them.

During each brief rest period they ate chocolate and raisins, but there was no time to brew hot tea, and it was a long time since their last meal before take-off at Malta. They thus suffered more than ever from the intense cold, which ate into their energy as much as the physical struggle of the climb. Conserving the supplies in their water bottles, they drank icy water from streams, but this chilled them and in some cases brought on stomach pains. From a psychological aspect, the cold appearance of the snow-capped ridges in the moonlight did not help either.

When they gained the summit of the ridge, they all had to lie still for a long time before they could gather enough strength to go on.

When the light of day strengthened, they came upon a ravine. At the bottom of it ran a boulder-stream racing with melted snow. There was also a small clearing with trees forming a screen towards the rim of the gully on both sides.

"Don't think we could find a better spot for hiding until nightfall," Pritchard said to Deane-Drummond. "What do you say?"

"It's ideal, sir," agreed the Lieutenant.

Scrambling down, the men set up their portable stoves and brewed hot, sweet tea. This warmed them up and raised their spirits. They boiled pieces of their pemmican ration into a thick, greasy porridge but found it extremely distasteful. Encouraged by the two officers, who pushed it down and made a pretence of liking it, they ate a little of it, because it was essential to take the highly nourishing substance to gain strength for the next night's movement. Some of the men, however, were quite unable to swallow a single spoonful, despite the fact that it was a very long time since they had had a meal.

In the hollow of the ravine they were sheltered from the icy wind that gusted over the mountains, and some of the men tried to sleep, but as the day wore on, this was found to be impossible because the coldness grew more intense even in their shelter.

Pritchard and Deane-Drummond consulted their maps and judged that they could not be far from the village of San Lorenzo. This did not worry them. But what did was their realization after further study of the maps that in the first night they had covered only about five of the sixty miles to the sea. On this fact the two officers had a private conversation, a short one.

"How on earth can we be only five miles nearer to the sea?"

"Well, many times we've had to make rather long detours."

"Agreed. In effect we must have slogged at least fifteen miles."

"I'd put it at that too. And the climbing was slow work – too damned slow as it turns out."

"What does it mean then?"

"It means we'll *have* to double the distance each night now in order to get to the sub in time."

"That's the way I figure it out too."

They discussed the fact that they *might* have a little extra time in which to make the journey. The Admiralty had promised them that, if they did not reach the mouth of the River Sele by the night of the 15th-16th, the submarine *Triumph* would leave and then make one more rendezvous on the night of the 18th. Their hope of getting there in time was negligible, but they did not tell the men.

Three hours after the day's rest began, the men became aware of the drone of a plane. It was a light aircraft, and it flew in low over the ravine, no more than five hundred feet above their heads. Quite clearly they could see a figure inside the craft looking down and using binoculars. They could not be sure whether the men in the spotter plane had seen anything to mark the spot as their hiding-place. But all realized that it was a probability rather than a possibility that the big search was on.

There was no more sleep that day, even for any who might have managed to keep warm enough. Many of them were now beginning to realize that Major Pritchard's name for them – guinea-pigs – was no light-hearted description. There was little doubt now that it was a guinea-pig operation. Some of them preferred to think of it as one to pioneer British parachuting. But both expressions came to the same thing. If the men had known, therefore, that they might be given a little extra grace by the sub *Triumph*, they might not have counted on it overmuch.

After the spotter plane circled and disappeared, the two officers, together with Sergeant Lawley and Henderson, climbed the banks of the gully and carefully peered out from the trees. They saw in the distance Italian peasants working in fields. Further afield, across a wide valley, they caught a glimpse of their old friend Calitri. The village clung to the mountainside half way up. It made a pretty picture in the morning sunlight. But the sight of it was somewhat disheartening, underlining as it did the fact that they had made so little progress during the night.

The scent of wild thyme and olive trees came to them on the morning breeze, but it brought no moment of pleasure, for they saw that ahead lay another of those muddy ascents, sheer and slippery cliffs, no less cruel than those they had climbed the previous night. Before them in the light of day terrain that would mean another climb as gruelling as the last. And to increase their apprehension, which must be suppressed at all costs, they had not unnaturally developed a hunted feeling.

Some time during the afternoon the men heard the shrill voices of children and the barking of dogs. Everyone kept quiet, willing the youngsters and animals to go away. It was a relief when the chatter and laughter passed away and did not recur.

Before dusk Sergeant Lawley again climbed the side of the gully. He saw an Italian driving a number of goats down the opposite mountainside. He made a mental note of the line of the goat track and suggested to Major Pritchard that, if they followed that during the night, they might fare better.

Darkness came. On went their packs, belts and pistols. Henderson shouldered his bren. Someone picked up the sub-machine gun. They scrambled up the slope of the gully and set off.

Soon they had to cross a stream ten yards wide. It ran swiftly and contained deep pools. Boulders formed a pathway across it. But there was a gap in the middle. All jumped this successfully except for one man who slipped and fell into deep water. Thereafter he had to march all night with wet clothes.

Lawley's goat track was not so helpful in the darkness as it had been to the herdsman during the day, and it was another dreadful ascent, knee-deep in mud. From time to time patches of scrub and long grass proved useful to help them to haul themselves up, but most of the time the ascent was as difficult and exhausting as that of the previous night. Attaining the crest, every man dropped and lay inert on the ground for ten minutes. Then they rose, formed into single file and marched by compass to a crossroad near the source of the River Sele. On the way they saw a cluster of cottages on the skyline. These, thought Pritchard, would be part of the village of Pescopegano. From that direction came the barking of dogs, of which the area appeared to have a large population. The howls did not help them to feel secure. The feeling of being hunted was now strong in every man.

Referring to their maps, they used a road as a guide, not marching on it (though this would have been speedier) but keeping it within sight about a quarter of a mile away as they moved towards San Andrea di Conza, which they skirted to the south, successfully crossing the River Arso by a bridge. Dry with exhaustion, they again drank from a stream, but they came across no more water until midnight, when Pritchard called a halt for tea to be made. Added to the exhaustion, the men's feet and limbs ached more than previously. The tea helped, but for the remainder of the night it was to be only will-power that would keep them moving.

Pushing on, they again kept the road in sight, and Pritchard noted that no traffic appeared to be using it, not a single vehicle, pedestrian or cyclist. He began to consider arguments for and against using the road itself on which to march. Certainly they would move quicker, put a greater number of miles behind them before daylight – a point for doing so, because they were still well behind schedule. Against the idea was the fact that, if Italian troops were searching for them, the roads would be used by them. Would they round a bend to come face to face with lorries filled with soldiers? Or suddenly meet up with a civilian transport and their presence be reported? Another point in favour of descending from the hillside was that they were leaving definite but unavoidable tracks, and those could be reported also. Would it be worth the chance of taking the road? He decided in favour of doing so.

He called a halt. "The road's deserted. I think we should take the opportunity of doing a spell along it."

Though exhausted, hungry, aching – in some cases sick, when they began marching properly on a hard surface and in military style, the men's spirits rose. They began to swing along, and for five or six miles they made excellent progress. Then they reached a crossroad and without warning came upon a hooded cart drawn by a pony, driven by a peasant woman with a brown, wrinkled face and soiled black dress. It trundled slowly towards them from the opposite direction. It was impossible for their presence to have escaped her attention – and that of another person behind her in the shadows of the vehicle.

"Come here, Trooper Nastri," Pritchard at once ordered. "March in front of us, as though you are in command of us. As we pass that cart, call out our step in Italian. Left, right and so on. If they call a greeting, reply in Italian. It's up to you to think of something innocent to say. Understand?"

"Yes, sir, perfectly," replied Nastri, moving out in front while the two officers fell back to form part of the column.

As he swung past the cart, Nastri cast a beaming smile on the driver. "*Buon giorno*," he called cheerfully.

The woman smiled and waved. The cart creaked past. The incident amused the troop. It also instilled a measure of confidence, and later, as they approached a village, Pritchard decided to risk marching through it to avoid making a long detour. He ordered Nastri to remain at the head of the column.

It was 4 a.m. The streets would no doubt be deserted, though there was the possibility of encountering a solitary villager out of doors. The village was in complete silence, indicating that no Italian search-party was present.

"If we come across a single soul, Nastri, do your stuff, there's a good fellow," urged Pritchard.

There was no sign of life in the village as they marched through. But they had just left the last building behind them when a farm worker was seen coming out of a field onto the road. He signalled to Nastri to stop.

"Out of the way, man, do not hinder us," shouted Nastri in Italian, keeping the pace of his stride and calling the step.

The column went on, passing the man, neither increasing nor slackening their speed. The fellow ran after them and fell into step beside Nastri. He asked questions. What regiment did they belong to? Their uniform was none he had ever seen in Italy, he suggested. Nastri replied curtly in Italian, hoping that what he had thought of saying would satisfy the men. They were, he said, Austrian troops on manoeuvre. The man smiled, apparently satisfied. But then he loquaciously invited Nastri to bring 'his men' to his house for a meal and some wine. Graciously the trooper declined and the column moved on, leaving the man who had accosted them behind. Later Nastri reported to the others the conversation that had taken place, and this gave place to groans and sighs.

"Just to think of it," they said. "A meal – and *wine.*"

"OK, OK," grumbled Nastri. "How much will power do you think it took for me to say no?"

Some men were almost asleep as they marched and afterwards had no memory of the countryside they had traversed. One was so dazed as to have been completely unaware of the incident of passing the cart or of the farm worker who spoke to Nastri. It would appear he had been marching automatically.

They continued following the line of the valley which took the River Sele through the Apennines.

When dawn streaked the sky, Pritchard called a halt for him and Deane-Drummond to study their map with a view to finding a likely place for the coming day. Some distance on there was a hill, and the map showed a fairly large clump of trees half way up it. That, they decided, was the spot to make for. They found the hill and began to climb it. They found the trees too. But there was something else very near to them that had not been shown on the map – a farmhouse. The men sank wearily to the ground and cursed softly.

"Back down the hill – fast," came the order.

Soon it would be daylight. And it was well on the cards that they would have nowhere to hide.

CHAPTER FIFTEEN

No hiding-place

Out came the maps again after the descent. They showed another hill a little further on named '*Cresta di Gallo*' – 'the Cock's Comb'. And it was crowned by a wood!

"We've got to go hell for leather to make that wood in time," said Pritchard. "We must be in its shelter before daylight, and we're going to be pretty pushed for time."

They struck west over the flank of a mountain in the direction of the hill shown on the map. They were fatigued, but they pressed on as quickly as possible. The ground was rising all the time and then, when they reached the hill, they were climbing strenuously. Just once Pritchard halted for a moment to peer upwards.

"Can you see any trees up there?" he asked.

"Can't say I can," replied Deane-Drummond. "But it's not quite full light, and I'd say it's a bit misty up there."

"Come on then, keep going."

They reached the snowline, and the soft squelch underfoot slowed their pace. At last they reached the summit. They looked all around them. There was no wood, not a single tree. It was unbelievable. For a full minute no one uttered a word. They stood still, staring. Had they chosen the wrong hill to climb? No man could bring himself to ask the question.

They stood in straggly line abreast, spread out somewhere near the centre of the summit. One of the men moved a little to his right, further away from his companions, and suddenly a shout came back from him: "Over here, sir." When the others reached him, he was pointing to a fairly large number of tree stumps, grouped together and none over a foot high. Realization of what had occurred came rapidly and with acute disappointment: at some time since the map had been made, the whole wood had been felled. In the growing light of morning, on the bleak, bare hilltop where their figures could be seen for miles, there they stood with no place to hide from the road below or from any aircraft that might be searching for them. It was too late to try to find a better place to spend the long hours of day that lay before them, movement now being more dangerous than staying where they were.

Up to then, apart from Daly's plane having to fly one man short and dropping its load in the wrong valley, plus some of the explosives jamming in the bomb racks, good fortune had been with them. Now their luck appeared to be running out, their chances of escaping from Italy greatly lessened.

All that grew on the hillside and its summit were a few small, stunted juniper bushes. There were not many of them, and they were well spaced out. They would afford only partial cover, and then only if the men were to lie down flat beside them. In addition, they provided little or no shelter from the icy blast of the wind. If they were attacked, there was not one boulder behind which they might make a stand. Hunting around, they found one small cave. It was only a few feet long and penetrated the hillside for no more than a couple of feet. No more than four of the men could squeeze inside.

The sky was clear and cold. Thin sunlight would illuminate their position. They felt like praying for mist and low cloud, but such good fortune seemed unlikely. Determined to remain optimistic, they held on to one remaining hope – that the nearest community, however small, was far distant from their hill and that no one would come near while daylight held. That hope too was soon dashed, for a reconnoitre to the other side of the summit revealed a village at the foot of the hill.

In these far from satisfactory conditions they must sweat it out for the whole of this second day. Or until something happened to induce a crisis.

They had no sleeping-bags and only one small blanket each to guard against the bitter wind that raked the bare, high scrubland and flicked at the snow that surrounded them. They huddled up to one another in an attempt to keep warm. But their clothes were soaked with sweat and became ice-cold against their bodies. Exhaustion helped to lower their resistance to the cold. They shivered and their teeth chattered. The few who had managed to get into the cave tried to light cigarettes, but these were wet and the operation did not prove successful.

With short rest periods they had been on the move throughout the night, but when the two officers consulted their maps, they found they had not been able to keep anything like a straight line towards their goal. All they could do was hope for easier conditions and greater progress on the third night.

Sergeant Lawley and one of the troopers took the first watch. It was 5.30 a.m. They sat down next to each other at one side of the cave. At first they talked to keep each other awake, but it was not long before they ran out of conversation, and they arranged that from time to time they would nudge each other to make sure they both were still conscious.

About an hour after the watch began, Lawley heard what sounded like a series of thuds, following each other at frequent and regular intervals. Whatever it was, it was from below and in the distance. Gradually it grew louder, and finally the sergeant saw what was causing the sound. It was a donkey. A pace or two in front, leading the animal, was a man, a tall Italian peasant wearing a dark coat and floppy, wide-brimmed hat. Lawley could see that they were traversing a winding mountain track which rose to a point not far below the summit and continued again downwards. The track would bring the Italian to a point uncomfortably near to them. If the sergeant attempted to warn any of the men, he would be seen more easily. Praying that not a man lying among the junipers would move, he nudged the other man on guard duty, pointed, placed a finger over his lips. Together the two placed themselves flat on their bellies, their heads raised to watch the Italian.

For an instant the Italian paused, glancing up in their direction, but immediately continued on his way, dropping down with the curve of the track towards the village below. Instinctively Lawley and his companion knew that the man had spotted them. He had studiously tried to look as though he had seen nothing. Lawley at once roused Major Pritchard, who sent Nastri running after the man. "Tell him we're Italian and German troops on manoeuvres," said the major. "Try your best to make him believe you."

When he returned, Nastri was far from satisfied with the way the conversation in Italian had worked out. It went like this:

"Don't be alarmed. We're a mountain troop composed of Italians and Germans, and we're spending a rest day on this hill."

"Don't delay me, I beg of you. I want to get home – down there." The Italian indicated the village.

"Just didn't want you to be alarmed."

"All right. All right. You have told me. I am sorry but I must go. I must get home."

"Well, as long as you know you won't be harmed in any way by our presence on this hill ..."

"Please, if you tell me you are Italians, then I will believe you. But please allow me to proceed."

"Certainly. A good day to you, sir."

"Thank you. Thank you. I won't tell a living soul I have seen you, and you will not be disturbed on this hill," lied the Italian. "Good day, sir." He hurried off, exhorting the donkey to its greatest speed down the track.

When the conversation was reported to him, Pritchard asked himself several questions. Had the man come upon them unawares? Had their arrival on the hill been seen by people of the village? Had their tracks been discovered in the snow by a shepherd out on the hills early in the morning? It was impossible to answer the questions.

If they left the top of the hill, either retracing their steps or continuing on in daylight towards the mouth of the Sele, they must be seen, not only by the villagers below but by others who would be about during the morning. And there could be worse points of vantage than the summit of that hill. Worse – but not much worse!

The men had not slept properly. Now they were completely awake. They did what they could to defend their position, though this was very little because of the total lack of cover and their limited weapon power. Corporal Henderson still had his bren; there was only one tommy-gun; they all had their pistols, but the range of these was limited, as was their ammunition. Pritchard posted look-outs to watch all approaches up the hillside.

Some time later two Italian civilians, armed with shot-guns, appeared on a ridge above them. No doubt by virtue of their knowledge of the locality, they had reached this position without being seen by the commandos. From this vantage-point they were able to gain a better view of the paratroopers than had the man with the donkey. They disappeared behind the ridge and were not seen again. Pritchard was now convinced that their presence was known, probably had been for a couple of hours. He ordered that all maps and papers be burned. In the normally peaceful village below there was great excitement. Warnings had been given out by the Italian authorities by radio and telephone that enemy parachutists had landed in their country, that they had committed an act of considerable sabotage and might continue to attack important installations. The civilian population, particularly those within a wide radius of the Tragino valley, were asked to keep a look-out for the presence of alien troops, who were described as probably being desperate men. The Italian authorites were amazed that a raid by enemy parachutists had taken place in their country. As far as they were concerned, it was the first such operation to take place in any country during that or any other war.

Early that morning the man with the goat who had passed close by Sergeant Lawley and his companion and had a brief encounter with Nastri returned, considerably shaken, to the village and reported that he had seen men in strange uniforms on the crest of the hill above their village. This was reported to the nearest *carabinieri* office. It was now believed that the whereabouts of the enemy invaders had been pinpointed. A message was sent to the village that assistance was on its way.

In the meantime a few farmers armed themselves with shot-guns and carefully approached the ridge to keep some sort of watch to make sure the enemy refugees did not move from the hill. Though two of the farmers were spotted momentarily, the others managed to keep themselves concealed.

In the village the news that "English desperadoes" were on their doorstep – or more accurately on the hill above looking down on them – spread like flames on a field of dry stubble. Excitement mounted further as cars and lorries began to arrive with a number of *carabinieri*, an armed and uniformed police force which had both peacetime and military duties, whose members were known to be specially picked men with better fighting powers than the average Italian soldier. They wore smart navy-blue tunics and riding breeches with a red stripe down the side, white bandolier belts and round military hats bearing the *carabinieri* badge of a flaming grenade. Automatic pistols hung from lower jacket pockets, and they carried rifles with bayonets folded back. In charge of them was a *sergente di carabinieri*.

Men also arrived from a mountain regiment, wearing leather gaiters and dark green uniforms with felt hats ornamented with a feather, and armed with small rifles with bayonets. These were also regarded by the Italians as crack troops.

This force assembled. Soon they would advance up the hill. Of the preparations below, the paratroopers on the hill could see little in detail but enough to make them aware that they were in trouble. It was difficult to realize that they were pinned down on a bare hilltop with no natural defences and an impossibly small number of weapons.

It was approaching the full light of noon, and the mountainside was bathed in a thin sunlight when the Italians came up to get them.

It seemed that whoever was organizing the operation down below had an uncanny knowledge of how the British would react to certain circumstances. The tactics employed were clever – if rather sly, and if the Italian in command wanted to make the capture without a single shot being fired, he was going about such a task in the right way to accomplish it.

First came three pointer dogs, sniffing their way up the slope. These were followed by what must have been the whole canine population of the village. Then came, unbelievably, a horde of children. Whether they had been sent ahead or were taking the lead excitedly could not be guessed by the commandos; the youngsters actually whooped delightedly as if setting out on a picnic. Next came the women! They toiled up the slope clutching their shawls and grinning like witches from the pages of a child's storybook. On *their* heels plodded the civilian men of the village. Last of all, well out of pistol or tommy-gun range, marched the Italian soldiery.

On the summit of the hill, spread out in a semicircle, stood Pritchard and his dozen men, each with a pistol in one hand, a grenade in another. Henderson was behind his bren-gun. Pritchard needed to give no order to hold fire. Who in that beleaguered little group would have pulled a trigger, for a single shot might have killed a child or a woman? Every weapon was lowered.

The crowd advanced upwards in an encircling movement, which made the paratroopers' dilemma even worse. There was no chance of fighting a way out. Quick assessments placed the oncoming crowd at about four hundred, including about a hundred armed troops. The British force was tiny by comparison, hopelessly outnumbered. But that was not the worst of it. How were they to shoot at the Italian troops without hitting the civilians who formed a solid mass in the forefront? Some of the men held grimly to a false optimism – that the order of the advance would change and that they would get a chance of directing some fire at uniformed targets.

To the paratroopers the tide of human beings flowed upwards with exasperating slowness. The waiting was dreadful, almost unbearable. They stole glances at their major, standing with legs apart, erect, almost immobile, his pistol raised, his other hand clutching a grenade. Their patience was severely tried as they waited for him to say something, anything to break the silence. But his lips appeared to be sealed. They did not like the look on his face. For Pritchard it was worst of all. There was a decision to be made, and it was the worst he had ever been called upon to make.

At last they were completely surrounded by a ring of women and children, not twenty paces away. Some of the children ran to within a few feet of them, staring at them with wonder and excitement.

"I think we've had it," Pritchard said slowly to the lieutenant, his voice even but strained. "I don't mean death. I wouldn't mind that if we could stand out to the last man. But how the hell can we show fight without harming the women and kids? What I mean is I'm afraid we're prisoners of war."

"It can't end this way, sir, not so tamely," said Deane-Drummond. "There must be something we can do. We've got *some* weapons. Do you think we could throw some grenades over the heads of the women and kids and far enough to scatter the soldiers behind?"

"Not a hope, Tony," Pritchard's voice was low. "They're too far away. The civvies and the kids would get it."

"And we'd be taken in the end?"

"Undoubtedly, but I wasn't thinking about that."

"Sorry, sir, but I'm not for doing just *nothing*."

A sound came from Pritchard's lips that Deane-Drummond thought might have been either a sigh or a groan.

"All right,Tony," said the major. "If you'll throw a grenade to the right, I'll lob one over to the left."

"And we'll kill some kids."

"And some women."

"All right," said Deane-Drummond. "You win, sir."

Pritchard raised his voice. "Listen to me, men. No one must attempt to fire or throw a grenade. Understood?"

There was no reply. It was as though an exploding bomb had stunned them. Only one man moved. Corporal Henderson, who in the end could not use the bren he had lugged so far, and as he thought for just such a moment as this, made a break for it. He hurled himself down the hillside, zigzagging as he ran. A group of *carabinieri* headed him off, and a number of farmers fired their shot-guns. When the *carabinieri* brought him back to the top of the hill, his hands were bleeding from pellet wounds.

The *carabinieri* came through the ranks of the shouting children and women, who were close in on the paratroopers, and surrounded them, covering them with their rifles.

The Italian sergeant shouted an order. Nastri translated. "He says we are to throw down our arms."

Angrily the sergeant, a heavy, portly fellow, repeated his order, waving his pistol menacingly while his men took another step forward, the muzzles of their rifles coming nearer.

"OK, men, drop your guns and grenades," said Pritchard. Not until they received his command did the men do so.

Pritchard found himself unable to drop the grenade he held. While struggling with the decision to surrender, though the only one possible in the circumstances, he had extracted the pin. He now held the grenade with the clip depressed. To release it would detonate the bomb.

The Italian sergeant stepped forward and jabbed his pistol at Pritchard's temple, shouting an order.

"What's the blighter saying, Nastri?" asked Pritchard calmly, holding on to the grenade.

"He wants you to drop it, sir," explained Nastri.

"Oh, he does, eh, the big fat goon," said the major wearily. "Well, listen, Nastri, try to get it into his thick skull that I've taken the pin out, and that if he doesn't clear a wide area so that I can throw it clear, a lot of people, including women and children, are going to get hurt."

All this time the pistol was still held at his head, the Italian's hand trembling with rage at the refusal to obey his order. For the paratroopers, particularly for Pritchard himself, it was quite a moment. At any second the unsteady fingers could have pressed the trigger accidentally.

Nastri explained to the excitable sergeant the dangers of the situation, adding: "I don't know if Italian soldiers get into trouble for shooting prisoners of war, but if that gun goes off in your hand, you'll have killed a British prisoner of war who holds the rank of major. He's in command of our company."

With that the sergeant lowered his pistol and shouted orders. These being obeyed, and the crowd having been shepherded to one side, Pritchard was able to hurl the grenade to a spot where it exploded safely.

Capture was bad enough. But worse was to follow – humiliation.

Soldiers appeared carrying chains, the sight of which at first puzzled the newly taken prisoners of war. Then, incredulously, they realized they were to be manacled. The long chain had handcuffs at intervals, and when the cuffs were clapped on their wrists, they were all chained together. Furthermore, each alternate prisoner was hampered by a large sphere of iron resembling an old-fashioned cannonball trailing on the ground from a separate chain. These they had to carry in order to make progress down the hillside. It was altogether incredible, almost as though the same equipment for prisoners was still in use as that centuries previously! Only Major Pritchard was spared the fetters.

Down the hillside moved the 'chain gang', and on all sides the crowd of civilians now mustered enough confidence to rile at them. "*Bastardo!*" they screamed. They shook their fists and spat at the British soldiers. There were other cries of derision which Nastri repeated in English for the benefit of his comrades ... "You will be shot ... You are murderers and spies ... You will be executed like pigs as soon as you reach the village ..."

Corporal Julian struggled next to Lieutenant Deane-Drummond. They carried one of the iron balls between them.

"This seems a bit like a three-legged race," quipped the corporal.

"I wish that's all it was," replied the officer.

"What d'you think is going to happen to us, sir?"

"Your guess, Corporal, is as good as mine."

The line of prisoners struggled to the foot of the hill. From time to time on the narrow winding track a man fell and was forced to his feet again with the help of a blow from a rifle butt. They were exhausted when they reached the village, where in the market square a further exulting crowd awaited them.

"*Viva carabinieri*," the Italians shouted. "*Viva Duce*."

On the steps of a building stood two men, and before them the prisoners were halted, One of them, a local dignitary of some sort, proceeded to address them, amid cheers from the crowd, and Nastri gave the gist of his words to his comrades.

"He says he knows we are the men who blew the aqueduct," said Nastri. The Italian said that the prisoners were murderers who had volunteered in England to become "*paracadutisti*" in order to get out of jail and come to Italy to raid their homeland. He added for good measure that he knew they were "English desperadoes" who were sent to Italy as spies.The other man took over the speechmaking. But he was haranguing his fellow Italians massed in the square. "He's trying to incite them to lynch us," Nastri told the man next to him, and this information was sent down the line.

One or two men, the braver element among the crowd, began to move forward towards the prisoners, shaking their fists. Behind them, one by one, moved others, and they were armed with knives, cudgels and hay-forks. Fortunately for the paratroopers, however, the *sergente di carabinieri* shouted orders, and his men closed round the prisoners to protect them. As luck would have it, the Italian sergeant realized that the prize he had taken from the hillside were his prisoners of war. But he had to shout another order before the crowd halted and fell back, this only when a volley of shots was released over their heads.

One of the two village dignitaries marched up to Pritchard. "Who is Italian in your party?" he asked in English. He pointed to Nastri. "That man. He is *italiano*, yes?"

"He's a British soldier," said Pritchard, "who happens to speak Italian."

"It is lies you tell," came the reply. "He has the face of an *italiano* – yes?"

"Nonsense," growled Pritchard, fearing for Nastri's safety. "You are an Italian who speaks English, and I'd say you have an English face. Are *you* English?"

"Do not insult me. I am not English."

"Well, that man isn't Italian either. Do you think I'd be foolish enough to bring an Italian here?"

"Probably not. You may speak the truth."

"Thank you." Pritchard treated him to a slight bow.

Though the conversation had ended satisfactorily, Pritchard's fears about Nastri were not stilled. Looking at the Italians all around him, he realized just how Italian Nastri's face looked.

The commandos were then locked up in a bare room with whitewashed walls, a red-tiled floor and barred windows. Between the bars from outside came a hand clutching a knife. It belonged to an Italian woman who for some time tried to strike them – to the accompaniment of chants from behind her suggesting that they should be executed.

Later an elderly Italian general came in, accompanied by a number of *carabinieri*. He addressed the prisoners in English. Smiling affably and assuming a soft, sibilant voice, he told them he admired them, that they were brave men and he had every respect for them. He then made an offer that appeared too remarkable to be sincere.

"Soon a lorry will be arriving. If you will give me your word of honour – you, sir, the major – that you will not try to escape, I will allow you to drive yourselves with no guard to the place to which you are to be taken. A car will proceed before you with armed troops and another behind you. You will follow the car in front of you. That I will allow for your bravery. I can do no more."

Pritchard remained silent.

"What say you, Major?"

"I say no," replied Pritchard. "If we are prisoners, I'd prefer we are treated as such. But I appreciate your offer, General, and I thank you." He felt he was one step ahead of the general, whom he suspected of planning to machine-gun them once they set off in the lorry under the guise of doing so while they attempted to escape.

Not long afterwards they were herded into a lorry – still chained together and well guarded by soldiers who made it obvious that they were looked upon as extremely dangerous characters – to Calitri railway station, within a few miles of where they had started two days before. They were placed in an evil-smelling waiting-room, again under guard. Dusk was falling when they were paid a visit by an officer of a Fascist militia regiment.

"I will not leave you in doubt as to your fate," he said in English. "At dawn tomorrow you are to be shot as spies."

CHAPTER SIXTEEN

A night ambush

Captain Lea and Second Lieutenant Paterson led their party from the scene of the shattered aqueduct on a compass bearing a little north of the one Major Pritchard had taken, the idea being to keep the parties to some degree separate though on the general line of the escape route.

They faced the same exhausting, almost impossible conditions and made no better progress. It had been the most severe Italian winter for many years, with a great deal of snow and rain and extremely low temperatures. Mountain streams that had been a couple of feet across had widened to six feet and more and were fast and deep, and they were fed by water gushing down from the hillsides to create waterfalls where none had existed before. In addition the rivers were swollen to many times their original size, and, like Pritchard's party, they had to make many delaying detours.

One fast-flowing river they tried to cross presented enormous difficulties. They waded across in single file, each hanging on to the pack of the man in front. One was nearly swept away. But Sergeant Johnny Walker, a twenty-two-year-old Scot more than six-feet tall and known as 'Big Jock', grabbed him and with difficulty hauled him back into line. What exhausted them more, however, was the deep, sucking mud. Often on the ascents they gained two feet and then slithered back three. Like the first party out, they used anything that came to hand to dig into the mud, giving the impression that they were paddling a canoe or poling a punt. Even for men who were in the pink of condition, who earlier had cheered as the aqueduct was blown, who had begun the long trek in excellent spirits, the task became disheartening in the extreme.

Captain Lea called a halt every two hours. Most of the party fell asleep almost at once, despite their sodden clothing and the bitter cold, only to be awakened in ten minutes to continue the appalling slog over the peaks. Always there was another ridge to conquer, one more fold in the mountains to traverse.

Lance-Corporal Harry Pexton was one of the cheerful extroverts of the party; he constantly joked and made light of difficulties. Perhaps that was why they called him 'Lucky' Pexton. The nickname often puzzled him, for on that and succeeding nights he was ready to agree with all the rest that they had been 'dumped' into an unenviable position. Often they recalled grimly that Tag Pritchard had described them as 'guineapigs'. The time came when Pexton's infectious cheerfulness waned and his quips became fewer. Like the others, he found himself pushing forward silently and automatically.

He and Corporal Fletcher, who were friends, had made sure they were in the same escape party. Discussing the hard going during a rest period, they recalled having heard their major utter a loud oath when his feet had stuck in the mud while setting off before them. "It must be the devil's own country if *he* let out a curse," they agreed. Pritchard was never known to swear, and they knew that he disliked bawdy conversation.

Trooper Jimmy Parker, a small, wiry Geordie from the north-east of England, often had a habit of grinding his teeth in his sleep. When he fell asleep during halts, his comrades noticed, he was too exhausted to do that.

Before dawn the two officers studied their maps to pinpoint a possible hiding-place for the coming day. They found that not far ahead on their route there was a ravine, and when they reached it, they were delighted to discover that it was clogged with trees and at the bottom was a dry river bed.

They brewed tea and prepared some pemmican 'porridge' but, like the others, found this most greasy and unpleasant to eat. After pushing it down, many in this party vomited and felt worse than ever, with the result that the next day they were to try to keep going on nothing more than their ration of raisins and chocolate.

The only dry place was the river bed, and they lay down there to rest. Despite the discomfort, they managed to gain a little sleep. Later in the day, when the sun rose high in the sky, they wakened with a shock to discover that water was washing over them. They judged that melting snow had made the river run again. Much of their gear was floating around them, and this had to be retrieved before it was washed away. On higher ground they lay down again in their sodden clothes. They heard aircraft overhead and guessed that a big search was on to spot them. The sound of distant lorries came to them also, and no doubt these were filled with troops.

Their exhaustion was such that there was little conversation. At times a groan, even a sob born of utter weariness, was heard.

Consulting their maps again, the officers considered they had covered no more than six miles. Fifty-four miles still to go. It was a daunting thought, and their only hope was that they would find the going better. With detours they must have hauled themselves a total of sixteen or seventeen miles but were only six nearer to their destination.

"It may sound like asking for the impossible," Lea told his men, "but I'm afraid we'll have to do better."

The next night they kept going by will-power more than anything else and at dawn were luckier than Pritchard's group on their second morning. They found a good hiding-place – a cleft in the rocks high on a mountain slope.

At about noon Bob Watson, Parker, Fletcher and Pexton were lying together concealed in a clump of bushes when they heard someone singing in Italian in a clear, beautiful voice. The vocalist was obviously very near to their hide-out. Cautiously parting the bushes, they saw a shepherd boy sitting on a rock surrounded by his flock of sheep. He was not twelve paces away. The four men lay low, making no sound.

"I hope for his sake the lad doesn't spot us," whispered Pexton. "If he does, we can't allow him to leave here."

They drew their pistols. One unsheathed his commando knife.

"If any of you lot could kill that youngster, I'm damned if I could," one of them confided later, putting his pistol back in the holster.

The others also put their weapons away. "We'll have to tie the poor kid up or something if he sees us," they agreed.

They recognized the song the shepherd lad was rendering. They knew it as 'The Ferry Boat Serenade'. For what seemed hours he sang it repeatedly, and the four paratroopers spent the time learning a number of Italian words by comparing them with their counterparts in

English. At last the boy rose and moved off down the hillside. His singing was replaced by the grind and drone of heavy motor vehicles passing on the road below.

That night they had been on the move for only an hour when Captain Lea had to stop. The previous night he had suffered agonies because his boots were ill-fitting. They were a pair of handsome mountain boots he had bought when they caught his eye in a shop window in Malta, and he cursed his impulse in buying them and dispensing with his Army issue. He tore the offending footwear off and slashed at them with his commando knife. When he replaced them, they were a little easier, though still painful, and he went to the head of the file and trudged on.

The previous night Lea had noticed that on the mountain terrain some of the men had lagged behind, unable to keep pace because of weariness. This was occurring again. He called a halt.

"It's a damn sight safer to keep to the mountains," he said, "but we're not making good progress. In fact, at this rate we'll get to the rendezvous long after the sub has been and gone, and this long haul will have been for nothing. I think the time has come to march on the road down there – and chance it. We'd get a move on – and we'd feel better."

"A bit bloody risky," some commented. "Do you think it might be better late than never, sir?"

Others said: "To hell with the risk. We've had enough of these bloody mountains."

Lieutenant Paterson agreed that Lea's plan was the lesser of two evils, and the decision to move down onto the road was made.

On the way down they found themselves suddenly in a morass. There was no way of guessing which were the deepest parts, and some of them sank to the waist and might have disappeared altogether in a death-trap of slime. Somehow they were dragged out and brought to shallower parts by their companions forming a human chain. They were fortunate at this stage not to suffer any fatalities. After their efforts getting through the dangerous swamp, they fell exhausted to the ground. They were not far from the road and in full view of anyone who might pass in a vehicle. Lying panting with the rest, Lea glanced at his watch. "I'm giving you five minutes, no more," he warned them.

When that short time elapsed, he hauled himself to his feet, accompanied by Paterson. "Come on, get moving," he said. His voice at that moment was no more than a hoarse croak.

"On your feet, boys." Paterson's voice was a little louder. "A good march now on a decent road. You'll just love it."

Either their training was responsible – or their characters, for they were all volunteers – for a rise in spirits as they began to march on the hard, level surface. In an hour they covered three miles and on the lonely highway encountered neither vehicle, horse, bicycle nor pedestrian. At a crossroad they paused and then put another three miles behind them in their bid for freedom.

A stone bridge lay ahead. This spanned a river. They would have to pass over it. But they could not see beyond it, not because of lack of light, for though the moon had deserted them it was not far short of dawn, but because it was a skew bridge with a sharp corner just beyond it. The bridge was sited in such a way that they had come upon it rather suddenly, and Captain Lea halted the men. They were some thirty yards from it.

"Stay here," he commanded. "I'm going forward to see what lies beyond the bridge. I'll wave you on if all is well."

He drew his Smith and Wesson from its holster and advanced warily. The stone walls cast deep shadows at each side of the bridge, but when he reached it, he found no sign of life on it, not even a stray sheep. He walked across it, turned the corner and found that it was deserted for at least half a mile. He stood listening. There was no sound save for a murmur of wind and a gentle rustling in the branches of trees at either side. The thought struck him that it was just a little too silent, but he dismissed the idea.

Returning to the bridge, he placed his pistol back in its holster and waved the men on. They moved forward. When the first man reached him, the last had reached the far end of the bridge, so that all were on it. And at that moment at Lea's end there was a rush of feet from the darkness of the trees that skirted the road. A motley crowd of civilians, men and women, a few armed with shot-guns, barred their way. They stretched across the road four or five deep. At the same moment there was a rush of civilians down the tree-clad hillside at the other end. At both ends of the bridge the way of the paratroopers was blocked. The Italians could not have ambushed them more neatly, and the brains behind the manoeuvre were soon in evidence as half a dozen *carabinieri* began to move in through the crowd.

The paratroopers drew their pistols. The man with the party's tommy-gun had it at the ready. With so many civilians around, they were faced with precisely the same dilemma as Pritchard's group. It seemed almost as though the Italian authorities had laid down a method of approach whenever any of the British intruders were sighted.

Lea cupped his hands with his mouth. "*Deutsch – Deutsch!*" he shouted.

There was silence. He repeated the words. No one moved. The commandos at the far end of the bridge from Lea turned to face the other crowd. The only movement there was by another half dozen *carabinieri* moving to the front. The paratrooper with the tommy-gun faced them. At his elbow Corporal O'Brien said: "Give the bastards a burst."

"How the hell can I?" was the reply. "I could mow the soldier boys down, but I'd take some civvies too. There are women there."

"They shouldn't be there."

"Well, they bloody are. The lousy Iti soldiers brought 'em along to hold their hands."

"Shall we let loose, sir?" asked a man at Lea's side.

"No," replied the captain. "There are a lot of civvies, men *and* women, and they've got us boxed in. We'll have to try something else."

"Try sounding like Germans," Paterson suggested, taking his cue from Lea and joining him in further shouts of "*Deutsch!*"

"Heil Hitler!" some bawled.

"Viva Duce!" others tried.

A *carabiniere* sergeant wearing a big dark cape stepped forward.

"*Inglesi, inglesi, inglesi!*" he yelled, presenting a rifle at Lea's chest. "You speak big lie. You *inglesi*. You all *inglesi*."

With the bayonet point inches from his chest, Lea drew his pistol. Holding the weapon at his side, he waited until the sergeant's tirade had ended. Then, quietly, looking into the man's eyes, he said: "*Deutsch.*"

"*Inglesi*," insisted the sergeant. "That uniform not *deutsch*. I no fool. We told of men marching. We watch you march for miles. We prepare to trap you, see?"

For this party, as for the others, the worst feature of their capture was the humiliating way in which it had been effected. The *carabinieri* were obviously determined to take the "English desperadoes" without a shot being fired. All the paratroopers agreed that they could not have been ambushed more effectively.

When the men were disarmed, the crowd of civilians began a tumult of shouting, and the paratroopers understood from the gestures they made that the rabble wished to dispose of them at once. No interpretation was required for them to gather what the *carabinieri* were being urged to do.

They were marched to a small village about a mile from the bridge, with the crowd screaming at them from every side. There they were pushed into the basement of what appeared to be a wine shop. They were then stripped and searched, though not very efficiently, as none of their hidden money or maps were brought to light. Watson, much to his anger, lost several large packets of cigarettes which he had strapped to his chest.

Handcuffed and chained together, they were loaded onto a number of mule carts. Escorted by *carabinieri*, and followed by jeering villagers, they were taken across country to the railway station waiting-room at Calitri where Pritchard's party were already imprisoned.

They had time to compare notes about the similarity of the circumstances of their capture before an Italian officer arrived and complimented them on having escaped capture for so long, as "several thousand troops" had been deployed to hunt them down. "You will be treated as prisoners of war," he informed them.

"Well, that's an improvement on their last announcement," Pritchard told Lea and Paterson. "They said we were to be shot as spies."

Asked by Pritchard how far they had got, Lea and Paterson said they judged they had been taken thirty miles from their destination at the coast. "We might just have made it if we could have kept to the road and not met anything," said Paterson. "But that would have been a miracle."

The prisoners were made to sit on benches all night. Every time they showed signs that they might fall asleep, they were struck with rifle butts.

"So much for our friend's prisoner-of-war stuff," said a voice in the dimly lit room. "I reckon we can't trust them a lot."

"I think we've got to face it," said another. "I'd say it's a toss-up what's going to happen to us."

CHAPTER SEVENTEEN

Trapped

"Would you like to join my group?" Second Lieutenant Jowett asked Sergeant Clements when the escape parties were being formed after the bridge was blown.

"I would, sir." Clements, the strict regimental sergeant, had a high regard for the tough, casual little Scots Canadian, and he answered promptly.

"OK, will you pick some men to make up the section?" said Jowett. "Oh, and by the way, Lucky's coming with us." Jowett did not bother to prefix the flight lieutenant's name with his rank.

Though the RAF man outranked him, Jowett was determined to command the party. The second lieutenant looked upon him as merely an interpreter or "some queer guy the War Office has foisted on us". (It must be said, however, that, though Lucky continued to be a 'mystery man' to the troop, there was probably more to him than was suspected. Some of the officers toyed with the possibility that his inclusion on the raid was an attempt to get an agent into Italy, though, intelligence matters being what they were, it was impossible ever to verify such a supposition.)

Trooper Ross, who had overheard Jowett's request, stepped forward. "Sergeant, I'd like to come with you if you'll have me," he said. The young wartime soldier, who had described himself as "Army mad", had an unshakeable confidence in Jowett, and Clements, the experienced regular, was to him the complete and perfect sergeant. Ross could not know, however, that the party he chose to join was to experience a nightmarish situation.

"You'll do, Trooper," said Clements. "Stand by me then."

Clements chose three more – Corporal Grice and Troopers Struthers and Crawford, the latter known simply as 'Jock' to avoid confusion with Sergeant Walker, another Scot on the raid, who was dubbed 'Big Jock'.

Under the shadow of Monte Vulture, soaring in the background, the party of seven set off on a selected compass bearing and, with the roar of water cascading from the broken aqueduct behind them, struck up their theme song – "Oh What a Surprise For the Duce". They did not sing for long, for from the start their battle over the mountains was as gruelling as that experienced by the other two parties.

Jowett and Clements discussed the arrangements for the submarine rendezvous at the mouth of the Sele.

"Tonight's Monday," said Jowett. "If we get to the coast by Saturday, that would be just fine."

"Do you think we'll do it in that time, sir?"

"Not at this rate. We're making progress like snails. I'll be damned if anyone could go faster in these conditions. But what you and the others haven't been told is that we may have about a couple of days in hand."

"How's that, sir?"

"Well, what you've not been told yet is that, if we don't get there by Saturday, we might be able to signal for it once more on the following Tuesday night. If we don't turn up on time, the sub's orders are to get lost and hide until the Tuesday night. Also, if all three parties get there on the Saturday and the sub considers it unsafe to take us aboard, it will sneak off, submerge and return for us on the Tuesday."

"Then we've got a chance, sir."

"Yes, Clem, we have. And we'll make it, you'll see."

Leading the party, Jowett set the pace. All the way the tough, wiry Canadian was at least a dozen paces ahead of the rest. From time to time he halted and gave them a brief and cheerful homily: "Come on boys, for God's sake try to keep up with me. I know I'm pushing it a bit, but I'm older than you lot." He was too. His bushy red moustache belied the large bald patch on the crown of his head, but no one ever established his precise age.

He placed Clements last in line, not only as a rearguard but to exhort the men from behind. "Push 'em on, Clem. Keep 'em going."

For Flight Lieutenant Lucky the test of endurance was worst of all.

He was in his middle forties, and that was old for such a slog, for the raid itself. But he kept going.

Though Pritchard had recommended that each party take only one sub-machine gun, this group was lugging two. Jowett had one, but Ross had saved another from burial in the ground.

"Good man," Jowett had said. "Hang on to it, if I'd had my way, I'd have taken one for each man. Five tommy-guns could do a hell of a lot of damage in a tight corner." Though none knew it, this party were to encounter just such a tight corner ...

The going was so rough that anything they carried eventually became heavier to hang on to, but Ross shouldered the gun and trudged on with absolute faith that they would get through. It never occurred to him that anything else could happen – not with Jowett and Clements to lead them. As the youngest man on the raid, he felt that anything that got in their way could be dealt with effectively.

Clements, older than he by some ten years, but very strong and fit, had taken part in mountain warfare in India, but he had never experienced anything so torturing and soul-destroying as this battle over the frozen Italian heights.

At early light they came upon a ravine massed with bushes. It looked just the place in which to lie low for the day. But when they descended into it, they found it waterlogged to a depth of about a foot. They could not chance going further, and they had to remain almost at the bottom to take advantage of the cover afforded by the bushes. Though at this spot there was no water, they had to lie in marshy ground with the chill striking through to their bodies.

Two of the men were moving trance-like, their eyes almost closed with tiredness, their feet treading automatically. It was difficult enough to avoid a dangerous fall with the eyes wide and the brain alert, and they were helped along by the others. These two slept soundly sitting in an inch or two of water, with their backs against the main branches of bushes.

Jowett pointed at them. "But for those two guys I'd have been moving on cautiously for an hour or two even in daylight," he said to Clements.

"So would I, sir," said the sergeant. "But we couldn't leave them behind."

"No, we couldn't," said Jowett. "They badly needed a rest."

Anyone who did not know the balding little lieutenant would never have guessed that he possessed unusual reserves of strength on which to call. All that day, and for others to come, his cheerfulness renewed the optimism of his men. No matter how much he cursed inwardly about the atrocious conditions, no one at any time during the bid to escape heard a grumble escape his lips.

Using their portable stoves, they brewed hot, sweet tea, and all managed to eat a portion of the pemmican ration. Crawford, the Scot in the party, had made sure of putting a bag of oatmeal in his pack before leaving England, and by mixing some of this with the pemmican while boiling it, the result was quite palatable. The men also digested the pemmican better. (Perhaps not even Crawford knew that a few centuries earlier Scottish troops could march further in a day than any others in Europe because the oatmeal they ate counteracted the unpleasant effects of pickled or raw beef on their stomachs!)

One unpopular order by Jowett was – no smoking. "We don't want to get discovered by blokes having a fag, or worse still smoking a pipe. Our stoves are special smokeless ones, so why spoil it?" Another order obeyed by all was that, if any of them became stiff and wanted to move about, they had to do so crawling or in a bent position so as not to rise above the tops of the bushes. The value of this became more obvious when later in the day spotter planes flew over their hiding-place.

With the dusk they moved out again and continued westwards. At 2 a.m. they came to a road which they would have to cross. Jowett, Lucky and Clements took a map reading and found that the road led to the head of the Sele valley, through which they might move on lower ground towards the sea.

Jowett stabbed at the map with a finger. "If we take this road, we can obviate a trek over the mountains. It's a longer way round, but I guess it would be a damn sight quicker."

"And a damn sight riskier," Lucky pointed out.

"Of course it's riskier," snapped the Canadian. "But we've not got a helluva lot of time, and we're in the business of meeting a deadline at the mouth of the Sele. I reckon the time's come for taking a risk."

The RAF man's face was grave. "From your point of view, yes. Perhaps not from mine."

"Why not?"

"I'm not in the business of getting caught with you lot."

"Meaning?"

"Meaning nothing. Forget it." Lucky's voice was calm, his statement final.

Jowett turned to Clements. "What's your vote?"

"I'm for taking the road."

Jowett turned an implacable gaze on Lucky. "You're outvoted, buddy," he said. "The road it is."

As they swung along the hard, even surface, Jowett and Clements were pleased to note that even the two most exhausted men were now bearing up and moving well. They were also puzzled about Lucky. On the one hand he was obviously keen to avoid capture. On the other, they sensed that there was no fear in him. But they quickly forgot the incident.

On rounding a bend they came without warning upon the first house of a village. It lay before them dark and silent. Was everyone in bed and asleep? It was a question no one could answer. On both sides the mountains rose bleak and barren, the peaks outlined starkly against the pale sky. To bypass the village would entail a great deal of climbing. To skirt the mountains they would have to go back miles.

"There's only one thing to do, boys," decided Jowett. "Walk through the village, but like bloody mice. Follow me and keep in the shadow of the houses. Sergeant, stay in the rear – and take Ross's tommy-gun."

His own tommy-gun in his hands, he set off at once. He went slowly, treading carefully. The street was deserted. But the utter peace, the night silence of mountain places, was unnerving. And the scuff of their boots, cautiously though they trod, seemed unduly loud.

They were half-way through when a dog started to bark. Its howls were joined by others, one by one, until it seemed that a dozen hounds were at it. The street was well lit by moonlight. Any villager peering through a window could not fail to see stealthy shadows crouching beside platforms like loading-bays which flanked some of the houses and creeping forward. Moonlight glinted on the two sub-machine guns. For the seven men it was not a comfortable moment. There was a sense of being trapped, not only by the houses but also by the towering mountains forming a sheer backdrop to the village. They had an urge to run. But Jowett kept stolidly to his slow, cautious tread, and none dared overtake him.

At last they emerged at the other side of the village, where they were thankful to find that the road immediately turned in a downward hairpin bend. Behind them the village was still drowned in silence, and Jowett, followed by the rest, broke into a run to place distance between them and the village. Soon they halted, out of breath, listening. Behind them was no sound. They had no means of knowing if anyone had seen them, but if they stayed on the road, any vehicle that set out from the village would quickly overtake them. New plans were now indicated.

They came upon a stream which flowed under a little hump-backed bridge, and left the road to follow this. Soon they were once again in difficult terrain, but as their maps showed that the stream ran into the Sele, they continued on. Coming to the river, they followed it but kept off the road which ran near to it. Later they took a short cut across country instead of winding with the river, their map showing them they could benefit by this.

It was still dark when they came upon a plantation of fruit trees. But soon it would be dawn, and it was decided that they should take advantage of its shelter for the coming day. They entered the trees.

Jowett was well ahead of the others, with Ross close up behind him, when there was a movement in the trees ahead, and they found themselves staring at a man who had appeared as if from nowhere and who stood facing them not twenty paces away. Wearing rough trousers, a waistcoat and collarless shirt, bald-headed and unshaven, he was no doubt a peasant farmworker. Jowett at once trained his tommy-gun on the man.

"*Buon giorno*," shouted the man.

"Stand still," ordered Jowett. "Don't move."

His English was apparently lost on the peasant, who moved remarkably quickly, vanishing among the trees as suddenly as he had appeared.

"I'll get him," said Jowett, tossing the gun to Ross and hurling himself after the man.

Ross had a pretty good idea what the officer intended to do, namely to put into practice what they had learned from Messrs Fairburn and Sykes at the Lovat Scouts' camp in Scotland. Jowett was cold-bloodedly aware that the innocent peasant would have to suffer if he caught him. He was determined no one must be allowed to give the alarm if it could be avoided, though what his action would be if he came face to face with the man again was not yet clear in his mind. The peasant, however, was fortunate. Searching among the trees, the officers soon found himself at a loss. His knowledge of tracking, which he had learned with his comrades from ghillies on a Scottish moor, was not equal to the skill the peasant showed in evading him. But the Italian no doubt knew every tree and bush in the plantation and had an obvious advantage over him.

Jowett returned. "Lost the bastard," he admitted. "Doesn't know how bloody lucky he is."

"He'll talk," said Clements.

"Sure he will. So we can't stay here. Come on. As far away from here as possible before full light – and fast."

They made their way through a narrow glen beside a stream, Jowett pushing the pace.

"I wonder if he's watching which way we go," said Clements.

"Just pray he didn't stop running," replied Jowett.

In view of what was to occur, however, Clements' conjecture was probably correct.

They followed the stream to where it flowed into the Sele, then marched alongside the river in the direction of its mouth in the west. It was well after dawn and lightening rapidly when they came to a wide stretch of the river in which there were a number of small islets surrounded by fairly shallow water. Some of these appeared to be well clothed with bushes, and as the mountains on either side offered little in the way of cover, Jowett decided to hole up on one of them. In the event it might have been better to take to higher ground and seek what cover the hillsides offered, but the bushes on the islands seemed in the half light to be thick enough to screen them, and rest seemed imperative instead of further climbing. They chose an islet which from the bank appeared to be quite densely covered with undergrowth, and waded across to it. They settled down to rest, but as the light strengthened, the leafless branches of the shrubs did not seem to offer the cover they had hoped for.

Jowett was uneasy about this and crawled to the other end of the islet. To his consternation he found he could quite easily make out the figure of his men even though they were lying down. His ultimatum to the men was this: "Afraid you'll have to lie flat and very still throughout the day. There can be no thought of cooking any food. You must eat biscuits and chocolate while lying flat and drink from your water bottles instead of going near the water. Sorry about that, boys."

They obeyed his orders to the letter. But about 11 a.m. they heard a dog barking. It was not far away. From where they lay they could see across the water to the river bank where the animal stood, its head pointing directly at them. In a few minutes a man appeared and stood beside the dog, gazing at their islet. The animal entered the water, swam across, landed and shook the water from its back. Then it ran excitedly among the men, barking and wagging its tail. It was not easy to remain inert while at the same time trying to shoo the dog away in low voices. The man on the river bank continued to gaze in their direction before calling to the dog, which made its way back to him. Its owner was not unlike the individual they had come across in the plantation, though it was not the same man. He made off fast, disappearing at the run behind the breast of a rocky outcrop in a direction which, according to their maps, lay a village.

"I'll go after him and spin him a yarn in Italian," volunteered Lucky, moving towards the water.

"Thanks, chum, but you haven't a hope in hell," returned Jowett. "By the time you'd waded across, he'd be a mile away."

"Do you think he saw us, sir?" asked Struthers.

"There's no doubt at all that he did," replied the officer. "We've got to get off this island – fast." He was already moving out, his tommy-gun held high above the water.

In one place there must have been a hole in the river bed, and as they waded across, one man stepped into it and disappeared. In his heavy boots, waterlogged clothes and heavy packs, swimming was impossible. With difficulty two of his comrades grabbed him and hauled him to shallower water, from which he waded successfully to the bank. Soaked from head to foot, he stood for a moment, a puzzled frown on his face.

"Where the hell is it?" He asked the question of himself. Then he turned to Jowett. "I'm very sorry, sir. I was carrying the other tommy-gun, and I must have dropped it when I went under."

"Hell!" said Jowett, but then attempted a grin. "Never mind, son.

Can't be helped now."

"Shall I go back and try to find it, sir?"

"Don't think you would, and in any case we've got to get a move on up that hill and find a different hiding-place. I'm afraid it's at the bottom of the river for the duration. But I've still got one."

They went up the hill as fast as their exhausted condition would allow. It took them half an hour to reach a height of about four hundred feet, some half way up the hill, and found a small clearing surrounded by shrubs, the only cover the bare hillside appeared to offer. But many of these shrubs, unlike those on the islet, were of an evergreen variety and better for their purposes than the ones below. From this point the ground fell for some distance before rising again to the summit, so that they were in effect on top of a mound.

"I suppose we could have been seen for miles climbing up here, sir," suggested Clements.

"Just what I was thinking," muttered Jowett. "But we'll have to hope for the best."

Ross dropped to the ground and went to sleep at once. Others lay down, panting hard.

Two hours passed before the silent valley came to life. A faint sound came to them as from a great distance. Eventually it was recognizable as the drone of motor vehicles, and it came from two directions, the east, from which they had come, and the west, for which they had been making. At last they came into sight, met and halted on the road directly below them, an assortment of cars and trucks which disgorged a crowd of men in civilian clothes. A rough estimate put the number at about a hundred. They looked like peasants and farmers. Every one was armed; most had shot-guns or sporting-rifles; some carried cudgels. All gazed up at the hillside on which the paratroopers were hiding; some pointed. For a time they remained in one large group, as though a council of war was being held.

"That bastard who saw us on the island has shot his mouth off," Jowett growled to Clements.

"Or the other in the plantation," said the sergeant.

"Or both."

"How bloody unlucky can we be, sir?"

"But how in hell can we be expected to sneak sixty miles in an enemy country without being seen, specially when they know we're around?" The look on the lieutenant's face was not pleasant. "Try to get to the top of the hill without being seen, Sergeant, and see if the way is clear at the other side. We might try a retreat down the other side."

Clements descended the other side of their mound and then crawled carefully up to the ridge which formed the summit, taking advantage of every bush and rock. Peering down, he saw an almost identical crowd forming up. When he returned and reported this, Jowett did not at first reply. He saw to his tommy-gun, making sure it was in working order.

"So we're boxed in like rats in a trap," he said. "Well, you'd better tell the men."

They looked enquiringly at Jowett, who ordered pistols to be drawn and Lucky to take cover with Grice, Crawford and Struthers facing up the hill while he and the others trained their weapons downhill. He himself crouched on one knee behind a bush with his tommy-gun.

"Now we wait," he said.

No one spoke, and the only sounds were the hill breezes and the cry of a mountain bird.

CHAPTER EIGHTEEN

Facing an execution squad

As if the Italians already surrounding Jowett's party were not enough, snaking along the winding mountain road came more vehicles, with every conceivable type pressed into service. There were lorries, trucks, waggons, horse-drawn carts, cars, even buses, all parked nose to tail in a solid ribbon on the highway. It was like using a steam-roller to crack a nut.

"Seems like half a division to take a few running foxes," commented Lucky.

"We should be honoured," said Jowett.

The new arrivals were mostly troops, and these were deployed on the far side of the road behind the civilian armed force and facing towards the commandos. A quarter of an hour passed while these preparations were made. To the beleaguered seven it seemed a great deal longer. For another ten minutes there was no further action. Then the troops beyond the road began firing up the hillside over the heads of the civilians who had spread themselves out into two long lines.

"I guess they know we're on this hill but don't know exactly where," said Jowett. "Reckon they're shooting to invite return fire. Well, let the bastards wait."

The Italians resorted to a new ploy. The armed civilians who had assembled began to move. They were spread out line-abreast, walking warily up towards the commandos and covering a wide area in two comparatively straight lines. 'X' Troop's raid had thus far accomplished something more than a shattered aqueduct – the beginnings of the formation of a civilian volunteer force to counteract 'invasions' such as this. The Italian civilians thus placed themselves in a military position and were fair game, as far as the paratroopers were concerned, to be fired upon. In this case there were no women, children or unarmed men. They were led by a man in *carabiniere* uniform carrying a pistol and walking a few paces in front. There were one or two further *carabinieri* among them, but they were mostly civilians. They were not shooting, nor now were the troops, who had advanced across the road to take up positions at the foot of the hill.

"The civvies look just like beaters in a shoot flushing game birds," suggested Clements.

"I guess that's just what they *are* doing," said Jowett, still crouching behind a bush with his sub-machine gun at the ready. Clements and Ross lay on either side of him, their pistols pointing.

Lucky, Grice, Struthers and Crawford did not take their eyes off a similar wave ascending from the other side. From its base the hill sloped gradually at first, then steepened towards a raised fold of ground. Thereafter it evened out and continued upwards more gently – towards the clearing. It took a long time – or seemed to for the three facing them – for the force to draw near.

Having breasted the first rise without being fired upon, the civilians began to display some bravado. They waved their assorted musketry and began to shout. Meanwhile the troops below them again opened fire, still able to aim above the advance in front of them. The range was closer, and bullets struck bushes which formed the paratroopers' screen, though their position was still not pinpointed from below. When they advanced further still, a hail of bullets would reach them.

The first line of civilians topped a mound below them. The centre of the line would soon be upon them. Jowett loosed a few shots above their heads in the hope that it would halt them. He was not particularly sanguine about this. The *carabiniere* who led them waved them on behind him, shouting an order. They still came on.

"That's just about far enough," Clements and Ross heard Jowett mutter as he lowered the muzzle of his gun. "If you can't take a hint, take this." The lieutenant fired three evenly spaced bursts of two. Three men fell, the *carabinieri* leader and two civilians. This stopped them. They turned and ran back down the hill, leaving the military to take their place, then taking the rear to follow the soldiers, who now ascended, making for the place from which Jowett, Clements and

Ross had fired, pausing every few minutes by order to direct their fire power at the hide-out.

Jowett turned to see the four defending the other side of the clearing firing their pistols. That they would be trapped between the two forces now seemed inevitable. He scanned the hillside at the other two sides. Some distance to the left was another patch of shrubs, some of which seemed from where he crouched higher and larger than those bordering their present position and forming a sort of small copse. It was sited a little further down the slope. He decided it would be a better place from which to make a stand. In any case, they could not remain much longer where they were, and if they made a break for the copse, they would be running fast downhill and might not present exceptionally easy targets. If the enemy had no machine weapons, that was.

He pointed out the patch of tall shrubs to Clements. "Tell the men to run like hell for that," he said. "You lead them. Tell 'em not to stop for a second until they reach it. I'll come last because I'll try to occupy them with the tommy."

Clements relayed the order. "I'm going first. Don't follow in a bunch. Make it singles. Each of you count ten before the next man goes."

Jowett moved to one side of their clearing, then the other, firing bursts at each but also trying to conserve ammunition so that he would not need to reload before he joined his men.

Running as fast as possible, the first three reached the copse almost before the enemy's eyes were distracted from the attention they were receiving from Jowett. The next three ran with rifle bullets striking the ground at their feet and whistling past their bodies. They all reached their objective and flung themselves to the ground. But the Italians now had their attention fully focused on the move, and whether Jowett would escape their fire was problematical. He realized this and took a different route. Bending low, he moved as rapidly as possible near the top of the mound, taking cover behind isolated bushes, then ran full speed directly down to the copse instead of diagonally like the others. He arrived uninjured.

Ross noticed that Crawford, who was lying beside him at the edge of the copse, had replaced his pistol in its holster, was clutching his right arm and muttering: "The bastards! The bastards!"

"What's the matter, Jock?" asked Ross.

"I've been hit in the arm," was the reply. The bloodstain was growing on his jumping-jacket. Because he was the last to make the run apart from Jowett, the Italians had been able to perfect their aim.

Ross examined the arm and found the bullet, or part of it, hanging on to a thread of the jacket. It had shed its nickel coat in his arm and come out of the wound. "A strange wound," he said.

"Och, man, they're bastards," said Crawford. "Are they using dum-dum bullets that split open on impact?"

Clements crawled over and applied a field dressing to the wound, but blood was still seeping through, and he borrowed some handkerchiefs, tied them together and bound them tighter round the arm.

It was not long before the enemy had completely surrounded the copse in a wide circle, still keeping their distance. Jowett, firing his tommy-gun, kept moving his position in an attempt to make the Italians believe they had more than one automatic weapon. Then the enemy began to move slowly in on all sides, and the other six commandos began to use their pistols, though these were not effective apart from showing an increased resistance. Crawford joined in, using his left hand.

The fire from the enemy became more and more intense as they closed in further, and the copse was riddled with bullets. It seemed a miracle that no one else had thus far been hit.

Clements crawled over to Jowett. "I wish we all had tommy-guns, sir," he said. "These .32s are useless."

"We're going to be taken dead or alive," said Jowett. "There's no doubt about it. Take the men out and surrender, Clem. I'm not having you all killed just for the sake of an operation that was bloody impossible from the start."

"What operation do you mean, sir?"

"I mean that, once we blew the bridge, escape was never possible. We never stood a chance. I knew that all along. Now get moving out with a white handkerchief for a flag, and don't wait for me."

"Why, what are *you* going to do, sir?"

"I'm not coming."

The sergeant, who had dropped his pistol ready to move out, picked it up again.

"So you'll stay and do what, sir?"

"I'm staying with this," said the officer, patting his sub-machine gun. "I don't fancy being a prisoner, but you'll all present yourselves as candidates for POWs — and that's an order. I've got two more clips left for this gun. I aim to use 'em, that's all."

"You'd not survive, sir."

"Maybe not, Clem. Maybe not." Jowett thrust his hand forward, and they shook hands. "Thanks, Clem, and thank the men for me."

The sergeant released his hand. "If you don't mind my saying so, sir, if you want to stay here, it sounds bloody silly. Bloody useless."

"Why?"

"Because if you're staying, we're staying with you. That's all."

"You'll defy my order, Clem?"

"In this case — yes."

The lieutenant rose to his knees and leaned his back against a bush, his tommy-gun across his knees, and Clements saw an expression in his eyes that looked like pain.

"All right, Clem," said the officer. "I'll come with you."

The noise of the bullets among the bushes was like torrential rain. Clements searched for a white handkerchief, found he did not have one and borrowed two from the others. "Bury your pistols and knives in the mud," he said, "and come out to join me when the firing stops."

The sergeant then rose and began to walk out of the copse, a white handkerchief held aloft in each hand. For fifteen or twenty paces the enemy fire continued. Bullets were hitting the ground around his feet as he walked. He was conscious of two thoughts, one that they were going to shoot him despite his surrender signal, the other that this was not possible. But at last the firing ceased altogether, and the only thing that broke the silence was the sound of his comrades coming out to join him. Last to come was Jowett, who had been dismantling the tommy-gun and pushing the pieces into the mud.

The armed civilians, possessed of a new-found bravado, took the initiative. About a hundred of them closed round the little group of paratroopers, brandishing their shot-guns, shaking their fists and shouting. They then marched the British party to each Italian who lay on the ground. Some were wounded. Three were dead. They were the ones Jowett had shot from their previous hiding-place as the advance first came near to them, and they included the *carabiniere* who had led them. The Italians pointed to the bodies, shouted at their prisoners, spat at them.

One of the civilians, hatless and wearing a brown lounge suit, a strutting little figure scarcely more than five feet tall, seemed to be taking charge of the situation as a self-appointed commander. He had two crossed bandoliers with ammunition across his chest; a non-military sporting-rifle was slung over his shoulder, and he held a small automatic pistol in each hand while two holsters were slung from a belt on the outside of his suit. He issued an order, and in the bitter cold the prisoners were roughly stripped of all their clothing down to the waist. Their pockets were emptied and their wristlet watches and rings taken. The paratroopers thought the little man might be a local mayor or civilian dignitary of some kind and that was why the military seemed to be allowing him to take charge.

Once the Italians had divested Jowett and Lucky of their jumping-jackets, they recognized them as officers by their badges of rank and kept the two apart from the rest, but on another order from "two-gun Ravioli", as Jowett christened him, all seven were marched to level ground near the base of the hill and forced to line up close together with their backs to an outcrop of rock.

"Two-gun Ravioli" shouted more orders, and twenty civilians lined up facing the prisoners, not a dozen paces away from them.

"I don't believe it," Lucky said to Jowett. "He's telling them they're a firing party."

"If you've got in mind what I think you have, you're dead nuts," Jowett called to him. "We're prisoners of war and must be treated as such."

The man, unable to understand English, looked blankly at Jowett.

"Tell him, Lucky," said Jowett.

Speaking Italian, Lucky informed the man that under the rules of war any thought of execution was out of the question. The 'master of ceremonies' swaggered up to Lucky, placed a pistol at the side of his head and informed him first that, if he did not keep his mouth shut, he would shoot him himself, then that in the case of English murderers rules of war did not apply so far as he was concerned and that he refused to listen to any arguments from the scum of English prisons. It seemed that the belief that the paratroopers were ex-convicts was fairly general.

The little Italian then retreated a few paces and continued: "Tell them to raise their hands above their heads. All of you."

"He wants our hands up," Lucky translated.

"Two-gun Ravioli" strutted up and down before them, delivering what sounded like a pompous speech. Lucky gave the gist of it to his comrades. "He seems to know all about the aqueduct being blown ... We have killed two civilians, not to mention the *carabiniere* chap ... He will take vengeance for the death of the civilians ... We are murderers and bandits and desperadoes ... He will not allow us to speak in our defence for we have no defence ... We can expect nothing else except to be shot like mad dogs."

The Italian's voice pitched high, and with mounting excitement in it his address became a harangue. He sounded not unlike a soap-box orator. Turning, he faced the firing party and the crowd of civilians, inciting them, drawing shouts of agreement with what he proposed to do. At his command the firing party put their guns to their shoulders and levelled them at the seven prisoners. They included eight- and twelve-bore rifles and one strangely resembling a blunderbuss. The voluble histrionics of the little orator began to hold the crowd in silence. Those wearing hats took them off as though they attended a funeral.

It was in fact an unreal situation, as though the seven victims were dreaming or taking part as actors in a scene being shot for a film. Better to have stayed up there and shot the hell out of as many as possible, thought Jowett. Clements told himself that, from the moment they set out on the raid, this sort of thing had always been on the cards. When they had left Britain and then Malta so full of confidence, had they in reality been setting off on what was sometimes termed a suicide mission?

The full reality of the situation had not yet quite penetrated into the consciousness of Trooper Ross, by far the youngest man on the raid. He turned his head towards the considerably older Sergeant Clements, the experienced soldier, who stood next to him. "What are they going to do, Clem?" he asked.

For a few moments Clements did not reply. "They're going to kill us. But don't worry lad. You won't feel a thing."

Ross was not a particularly religious chap. He said no silent prayer. He just said to himself: "Goodbye mum – goodbye dad." He looked at the faces of the others and saw that not one showed any trace of emotion.

With one arm he was supporting the sagging weight of the wounded Crawford. The other he had to keep aloft. But he wanted to use it to prevent his trousers, already slowly slipping down to his thighs because his belt had been taken away, from falling to his ankles. His mind became mesmerized with the thought that he might have to face death with his trousers around his ankles. That would be undignified.

"He's talking to the firing party now," Lucky said. "He says he will raise his arm and when he drops it they are to shoot to kill."

The organizer of the execution moved to a spot beyond the end of the line of marksmen and a little in front of them. He raised his arm. He kept it there, as suddenly he must have thought up a new twist to his oratory and continued his self-satisfying declamation. He paused. The silence was intense. The sun was bright, dazzling, but it was a cold light. A chill wind swept down the valley. The crowns of snow on the mountains sparkled. In the silence the seven men thought they heard a faint thudding in the distance, as if from the right. It must be imagination. Some of them thought it must be the sound of their own heart-beats somehow throbbing in their heads.

The man with his arm upraised was enjoying himself too much to hear the sound. His arm began to drop, but it was raised to full height again as he spoke again, this time in a monotone as though intoning a prayer.

The victims realized suddenly that the thudding sound was real. They risked moving their heads an inch or two to the right and saw that a horseman was riding hard towards them.

He was an Army officer in a smart blue-grey uniform with riding-breeches bearing a royal-blue stripe down the side, peaked cap, Sam Browne belt supporting a pistol, black riding-boots and a cape lined with royal blue billowing out behind him. He was spurring his horse, a big chestnut, to a gallop and pointing with his arm extended forward as if he were leading an old-fashioned cavalry charge.

"*Militari!*" They could just catch the word he was shouting.

The hand of the self-appointed executioner began to fall. The firing party could now hear distinctly the officer's shouts.

"*Militari! Militari!*" They hesitated.

"Fire!" shouted the cocky little Italian.

Realizing what was afoot, ignoring his own danger, the officer rode on and halted his horse directly between the firing party and the prisoners. No shot was fired, and the rifles were lowered.

Leaping from his horse, the officer strode up to the would-be executioner and with a gloved hand struck him violently across both sides of the face. Thus humiliated, the bumptious little fellow became the subject of another harangue, this time a severe dressing-down.

The Italian officer then turned to the prisoners and spoke to them in English.

"You have nothing to fear. I have pointed out to this my fellow countryman that he had no right to interfere with you in any way. It is not a civilian matter. You are the Army's responsibility. You are prisoners of war and will be properly treated as such. This he now understands. This all of the people here now understand. You are to be taken to a village some miles from here, and I have given orders that, apart from being guarded, you are not to be interfered with."

The officer cantered off, and within a few minutes a company of some twenty Italian soldiers took charge of the prisoners.

Crawford collapsed altogether, slumping to the ground. Ross bent down to pull up the offending trousers which had by that time fallen down to his ankles.

CHAPTER NINETEEN

"The beautiful Englishman"

News of the Italian officer's anger at civilians taking the matter into their own hands spread quickly among the crowd, which rapidly dispersed. The prisoners did not again see "Two-gun Ravioli".

As the vehicles left the scene, Jowett and his men had their uniforms returned to them and were made to walk to the village surrounded by their guard with a sergeant in charge. A few of the bolder civilians followed in their wake and began to jeer and throw stones. But the sergeant obeyed his officer's order to the letter, angrily putting a stop to such behaviour. He also detailed two of his men to support the wounded Crawford, who was by this time very weak indeed.

At the entrance to the village, however, another unpleasant scene took place. There a further crowd of civilians awaited them, including a man who appeared to be principal citizen of the place. He was a thick-set, paunchy individual, and he sat on a stone wall wearing a huge belt full of cartridges. In his hand was a Mauser pistol, and this he kept putting to his head while pointing to the prisoners to indicate what he expected or hoped would be their fate.

They were taken to the local *carabinieri* headquarters and told to sit on a wooden bench. The man with the Mauser followed them inside, placed the muzzle of the pistol at Jowett's nostrils and shouted excitedly, then repeated this performance with each of the other prisoners. He appeared to give an order to the Italian sergeant, waving his pistol first at the prisoners and then outside, repeating a word over and over again. "He's saying 'shoot'," said Lucky. The sergeant, who did not seem to share the excitable temperament of his fellows, studiedly ignored him but later jerked his thumb towards the door.

Taking the hint, the fat Italian put his pistol away and left.

"We'll have to get Crawford attended to," said Jowett. "See what you can do, Lucky."

Lucky asked the sergeant for help for the wounded man, and a doctor was brought. He asked for a large glass of whisky to be produced, ordered Crawford to drink half of it, extracted pieces of bullet from the wound and dressed it.

Crawford glanced at Ross and noted that his face was a pale shade of green. "Drink the rest of that whisky," said Crawford. "I think you need it as much as I do."

Ross emptied the glass and some colour returned to his face.

They were taken to spend the night under guard at a house in the village. Only Crawford was given some food, an egg and a piece of dry bread.

By this time an army captain was in charge of the guard.

"I give you chance for exercise," he told Jowett in English. "You are commander of your party, yes? If you give word of honour, you and your men may go out in street without guard to walk, eh?"

"I thank you, Captain, and appreciate your offer," Jowett replied. "But I'm afraid I must decline. As you must appreciate, if we were to leave this house, it would be our duty to try to escape."

Like Pritchard, who had been given a similar offer, Jowett feared it might be a trap whereby they could be dispensed with under the ploy of pretending they were trying to make off. Jowett could have been wrong, but he was not going to risk it.

The next morning they were given gruel for breakfast, after which the captain pointed to Ross, the only member of the party who had very fair hair, and announced that the women of the village had asked to be allowed to see "the blond Englishman".

"They live here all their lives," the captain explained, "and never before do they see a man with blond hair. Are you what I think you English call 'game' to do it? For the women it would be, I think, something in the memory for all their lives."

"I'm not crazy about being on show," said Ross.

"Oh, go on, Ross, give 'em a break," smiled Jowett. "You can tell your grandchildren that the women of Italy fell for you in a big way. And besides, it might be good for public relations after all the crap that's been thrown at us."

"You will do this thing?" asked the captain, smiling broadly.

"Oh, all right then," agreed Ross, "but it seems daft to me."

The captain escorted the youthful trooper to a veranda at the front of the house, where a crowd of women gazed at him for a time and then called to the officer.

Lucky laughed. "They're telling the officer they are going home to brush their hair and put on their best clothes to return again to see the beautiful Englishman later in the morning. At 11 a.m. Ross was again paraded on the veranda to satisfy the curiosity of the womenfolk.

The women had become more friendly, but not apparently the men. An army truck arrived in the village square to take the prisoners away. They sat on seats with their backs bulging behind the canvas top of the vehicle, which was surrounded by a crowd of peering men. Suddenly they heard a loud shout in good English. "Get your backs away from that canvas!" It was the voice of Lucky, who had been trying to discover their destination from an Italian sergeant before boarding. When he entered the truck, he explained that he had heard a number of men armed with knives saying they would stab the parachutists through the canvas.

There were guards in the truck, and another filled with soldiers followed it closely while a third preceded it. Their destination was Calitri, where they were shepherded into a railway station waiting-room. Sitting languidly on benches, or lying bored and unhappy on the floor, were all the members of the other two escape parties.

Clements halted in the doorway, gazing at them unbelievingly. "So none of us got away. I thought perhaps one ..."

Emotion does not need to be divorced from bravery, or even toughness. Clements had his fair share of all three. He rarely showed the emotional part of his make-up. But this was one occasion when he did. If only one of the parties had got through to the coast, the total disappointment of this moment might have been averted, and for him the whole raid would have been more meaningful. The sight of Pritchard's and Lea's parties already in captivity did for the emotional sergeant what danger and action had not. Heavily and wearily he sank onto a bench. For some ten minutes he did not trust himself to speak. And any who looked closely at him saw tears glistening in his eyes.

At this time Clements did not take Captain Daly's party into consideration. It was believed that something worse than dropping in the wrong place had happened to them.

Daly and his four men were in fact then still on the run.

After being dropped in the wrong valley, they spent the rest of that night making for the rendezvous. They took a compass bearing and climbed up and over a mountain in the same daunting and difficult conditions as those experienced by the other three parties.

With one mountain behind them they came upon tracks in the mud and snow and decided that they could have been made by one of the other escape parties. Daly consulted his map and set a new course, which was to prove a good one.

At one time finding themselves up to the waist in snow, at others in deep mud, it was almost impossible to make any progress at all. But later their route led across more solid ground, and when daylight came and they found a wooden hut in which to shelter for the day, Daly was quite pleased with the distance he judged they had covered. On their chosen route they kept going for a further three nights. Nothing except the difficulty of the terrain and their exhaustion kept them back, for as luck would have it, they came upon no village or habitation of any sort.

Only on the third day, when they holed up in a small wood, did they see some distance away a very lonely farmhouse. During the day they crept near to it, and because of its complete isolation Daly and one of his men risked walking boldly into the farmyard where a man and woman were standing. "*Cibo*," they kept repeating, believing that the word meant food. But the two Italians hurried into the house and proceeded to shut and lock all doors and windows.

"OK," said Daly, "back to the pemmican ration."

Once during the next day they saw from their hiding-place a party of *carabinieri* marching along a road quite near to them. One of Daly's men levelled his pistol at the squad. "We could make quite a hole in that lot, sir," he said.

The captain put a hand on the barrel and pushed it downwards. "Put the thing away, you fool," he said. "Our job is to remain completely hidden. We've managed that for days. Don't spoil it now."

By dawn on the 15th they were looking down on what appeared to be a coastal plain. They were in fact only eighteen miles from the mouth of the Sele. They of all the four parties looked like making the submarine. But they had to get there by that night if they were not to hold up the submarine, and for all Daly knew, the others were also making good time. Thinking this, and taking into consideration the fact that they had come across so few signs of life, Daly decided to risk marching on during daylight.

As the light grew, they came out from the shoulder of a hill and found a deserted road before them. Checking on his map, Daly found that it went directly to the sea.

"We're on the last lap," he told his men. "It's all or nothing now, so we'll take that road and move fast."

All went well until about 11 a.m., when they rounded a corner and walked straight into a full company of Italian soldiers taking a rest on both sides of the road during a route march. The five paratroopers drew their pistols. But at a word of command from an officer who recognized their muddy and bedraggled uniforms as British, the Italian soldiers leapt to their feet and had them surrounded in a moment. And to make matters worse the people around them included a party of civilians who had followed the soldiers from a nearby village as they marched through. Jowett's party alone had not had to contend with the presence of women and children!

There was no interpreter in the party, and Daly began speaking in German, a language he had not used since his schooldays. They were, he told the officer, the crew of a German plane which had crashed in the mountains and they had parachuted to safety. The Italians asked where the plane crashed. Daly jerked his thumb backwards. It looked as though his ruse was working. In a high-handed manner Daly then said it was of the utmost urgency that they reach Naples by 2 p.m. and a car must be provided for them.

The Italian officer was smiling, but as it turned out sarcastically and in triumph. "I have seen no German wearing that colour of uniform, either Wehrmacht or Luftwaffe," he said in English. He then pulled Daly's jumping-jacket clear of his shoulder to reveal the three pips on his epaulette. "As I thought," he said. "Stars on the shoulder. They are English stars."

There seemed no suitable reply to make, and Daly remained silent.

"Your pistol, *Capitano*, if you please," said his captor. "Your pistols all of you, and you will submit to be searched."

The grenades they carried in their trouser pockets were also taken, and they were marched back the way the Italian company had come, to a village square, where the officer laughing told the mayor that they had pretended to be Germans who had parachuted from a crashing plane.

"*Paracadutisti,*" said the mayor. "Not German *paracadutisti. Inglesi*! Of the *paracadutisti* at Tragino I 'ave learned."

Daly and his men were handcuffed and chained and taken by army truck to Naples. They had nearly made it to the coast.

Not one of the thirty-five men who had parachuted into the Tragino valley had managed to escape. Every one was a prisoner.

CHAPTER TWENTY

Rescue plan cancelled

At Naples the last group to be captured were taken to a civilian prison, and Captain Daly was separated from his men and placed in a cell by himself. They were not at first interrogated, the Italian authorities believing correctly that all the men involved in the raid had now been taken and that there was time enough to conduct interviews when the whole party were together in one prison.

The Italians' main worry was that such a raid had taken place at all. Not surprisingly, at no time during the war until then had Italian commanders visualized such an attack, and that enemy parachutists had landed and committed an act of sabotage before their presence was known seemed to them almost incredible. Both the Italians and the Germans had been aware of the possibility of attacks on the coasts of Italy or elsewhere in Europe by seaborne commandos, but neither of the High Commands had visualized until then the possibility that British paratroopers, who they did not know existed, might be dropped into their territories at all, still less that they could penetrate so far inland. Even the Germans, who had formed a parachute regiment before the war, used it only inside Europe, and not on a wide scale, in the early days of hostilities before the fall of France. So, when the news of 'X' Troop's assault on the Tragino aqueduct reached the Nazis, they were equally shocked.

Eventual interrogation of those who had taken part in Britain's first-ever parachute drop into enemy territory was to be aimed at trying to discover if further such raids might be already planned by Britain. In Italy plans were already being made to warn both the military and civilians of the new danger from the air, and orders were given for closer observation of enemy planes in order to report any sign of descending parachutists.

Alone in his cell, Daly was left very much to his own thoughts, and these were taken up almost entirely with the unhappy belief that his party alone had been captured and that the remainder of 'X' Troop had been ahead of him and had already reached the coast.

If he could find some means of escaping, he thought, there might just be time to join them before HMS *Triumph* made its last rendezvous after the weekend and then submerged to make for Malta. At a very rough estimate he might have some forty miles to go with little or no climbing, for the mountain ranges rising to six thousand feet and more over which he had already struggled lay inland. At this time the memory of those climbs was fresh in his mind. He recalled the exhaustion, the snow-filled ravines, the frozen wastes where at times it was difficult to breathe, the morasses in which they had sometimes swallowed mud and vomited. He realized that he would have to encounter extraordinary good fortune to make the submarine in time. *If* he escaped ...

But he also decided that it was his duty to escape, whether he ever reached the mouth of the Sele or not. One idea he thought would be to try to jump on a goods train towards the Sele and thus quicken his journey. There must be railway routes out of Naples. He began a close investigation of his cell in the hope of finding some way of getting out. The window was securely barred and in any case was too high to reach. He paid particular attention to the huge oak door. It was bolted on the outside. He found a hole in it just large enough to wriggle his finger. He made a mental note of this, and when he was taken out of the cell to be presented before the prison governor, he glanced backwards as he left and saw that the hole in the door came out near to the bolt. Was this his big chance? He experienced a thrill of optimism.

His appearance before the governor was brief, and on his return to the cell he waited impatiently until nightfall before inserting his finger in the hole to work at the bolt from the inside. Many times he tried to ease it without success, but with patience and perseverance he at last got it to move and the door opened.

There was still the guard room between him and freedom, and he hid himself among empty boxes piled against it. He was plagued with fears that at any moment his cell might be found to be empty. Eventually there was a call from inside the guard room, and the guard at the entrance entered the room for a moment, giving Daly a chance to slip past unnoticed. He roamed the darkened streets of Naples, wishing he could speak Italian in order to ask directions to the railway station. As luck would have it, he heard the noise of engines and, making in that direction, came upon a railway goods yard. There he waited until a goods train began to move out. Running forward, he attempted to board it as it gathered speed, but as he made his leap his hand missed the bar which he was attempting to clutch. He was thrown back on the track and knocked out by the fall.

When he came to, a group of Italian soldiers were staring down at him, and a rifle with bayonet fixed was pointing at his chest. They took him back to the prison, where he was placed in the same cell. But the hole in the door was effectively stopped up and the bolt better secured.

Had Daly or any of the others reached the mouth of the Sele, their terrible trek over the mountains would have ended in nothing but disappointment. There would have been no answering call to the signals they sent out across the water.

This would have been explained away as being due to what happened to one of the two Whitleys that had carried out the diversionary bombing raid on the night Pritchard's company left Malta.

The plane in which Commander Sir Nigel Norman flew to observe the paratroops descending at Tragino dropped its bombs on the railway yards at Foggia, causing explosions and fires. Later, passing Sicily on its way back, it released its last bomb above a railway and returned on schedule to Malta and thence to England.

But the other Whitley ran into bad luck. This was S for sugar No. N1456, skippered by Pilot Officer Jack Wotherspoon, from Burnley, Lancashire. His crew were Sergeant Pilot (later Flying Officer) Fred Southam, aged twenty-one, the second pilot, Sergeant Observer (later Squadron Leader) Harry Meddings, aged twenty-four, Sergeant Basil Albon, aged twenty, the wireless operator, and Sergeant Eric Hodges, the rear gunner.

S for Sugar bore on its nose as its mascot a metal figure of a half-naked woman presented by the *Daily Mirror* and representing that newspaper's strip-cartoon character Jane. It accompanied Norman's plane until, flying at four thousand feet, the port engine suddenly seized up. It lurched violently, and the crew expected it to go into a spin, which Wotherspoon knew would be difficult to correct at that height. In the event, the aircraft dropped only five hundred feet, and Wotherspoon was able to regain control and announce that one engine had gone and that he would try to get back to Malta on the other. He ordered that the bombs be jettisoned and turned for Malta. But within five minutes the other engine was found to be overheating because of loss of cooling-liquid.

Wotherspoon ordered his crew to abandon the aircraft. Only one had ever before made a parachute jump. Like other RAF crews they looked upon their parachutes as being for an emergency that might never arise. Hodges had, however, once baled out on an operation, and he told the others there was nothing to it, that one just jumped and pulled the rip-cord and left the rest to other things, including gravity. He went on to explain that, if the parachute had been properly packed, a piece of red cotton should be observed when one lifted the flap. All examined their parachutes, and most found the piece of red cotton, though Southam was disconcerted to find no trace of it on his.

Wotherspoon was to make an extraordinary decision. Neither he nor any of the crews of the Whitleys taking part in the raid knew about the plan for a submarine to lie off the mouth of the Sele to rescue the saboteurs. This information was guardedly given only to Pritchard and his officers, the command of the *Triumph* and a few members of the naval staff at Malta. Yet it is unbelievable that by sheer coincidence Wotherspoon, having studied his map and consulted his navigator, decided that the sandy mouth of the Sele was the best place for him to attempt a forced landing. In addition, he ordered a message to be radioed to base at Malta that this was his intention, due to engine failure. The message also stated that he and his men would lie up at this very spot in the hope of rescue. What he had in mind was to hide there for about five days before thinking of fresh escape plans.

Records show that those in command at Malta reckoned on the possibility that Wotherspoon's signal might have been picked up by Italian listening services and that it was not impossible for the enemy to decipher the code S for Sugar had used.

I can understand these two possibilities entering the mind of those who waited in Malta for Pritchard's trek to come to an end and the planes employed to return to base. Similarly, I can appreciate that it may have been feared that Italian soldiers and police might be despatched immediately to the mouth of the Sele to capture the Whitley's crew. (In the event this is just what did take place. The Italians did find and capture all those who baled out of the crippled plane and Wotherspoon himself, who crash-landed safely in the sand at the mouth of the river.) Nevertheless, I find it difficult to understand why for this reason alone Pritchard and his men were left to their fate. Wotherspoon and his crew were found and taken away from the area days before the first of the paratrooper fugitives could be expected to reach the spot. The crew of S for Sugar could surely have been counted on to say nothing, even under interrogation, about the existence of the paratroopers, and in any case they were completely ignorant that the commandos were to make for the mouth of the Sele. If they had gone beyond giving name, rank and number, surely their story would have been only that they had been on a bombing raid.

If the submarine had arrived days after the bomber came down, to take off the paratroopers, it is also to be expected that its commander would have done so with all necessary caution.

It is true that, as it happened, there would have been no one for the submarine to rescue, for none of the four parties reached the rendezvous at all. One is left, however, with the suspicion that perhaps Pritchard and his men were never expected to reach the coast after blasting the aqueduct. Was their role, therefore, that of guinea-pigs from the start? The thought that this might have been the case is inescapable.

It is certainly a fact that HMS *Triumph*'s sailing orders were countermanded. She never left Malta.

CHAPTER TWENTY-ONE

No hope for Picchi

The Italian general who visited the railway station where all parties except Daly's were held made a speech commending their bravery.

"You parachute into the heart of our country and commit a great act of sabotage," he said, speaking good English. "You must have known that you would never get out of our country again. Your superiors who sent you must also have been aware that the worst you could expect was to be killed trying to escape and the best to become prisoners of war. To have escaped would have been a miracle – and miracles do not happen in war. So, you are brave men.

"I am a soldier – and I appreciate bravery in any man, either one of my own or an enemy. I will make it my personal responsibility that you are treated with honour and in all respects as prisoners of war according to international rules."

Pritchard had risen to his feet in politeness because of the man's rank, and his men had followed suit. He stepped forward.

"That being the case," said the major, "I ask that my men be given food without further delay. They have had no proper meal for three days."

"Why have these men not been fed?" the general asked one of the officers of the guard.

"They not say they are hungry," was the reply, "and there was much to do."

"See that they are fed adequately – at once," ordered the general.

Within minutes of his departure the paratroopers were brought bully beef and bread. The meal seemed to them the best they had ever had.

The general's visit was to prove fortunate in another way. Soon after they had finished the meal, a party of Fascists wearing black shirts arrived and their leader demanded that the prisoners be handed over to them. A *carabiniere* officer refused the request in Italian, and Lucky later reported the dialogue:

"You will not disobey *my* authority, which comes direct from the Duce."

"I have *my* authority from a general of the military. He says they are to be treated with honour as prisoners of war. I will obey that order and no other."

"I suggest you think carefully and hand over the *paracadutisti*. Otherwise it will go ill with you."

"And *I* suggest you leave at once or it will go ill with *you* when this comes to the general's ears. These men are prisoners of war and under my jurisdiction. Go this instant or I will send a message to the general, and it is you who will be in very great trouble."

The man in command of the Fascists turned on his heel and strode out of the waiting-room, followed by his companions. They were never seen again.

The next day the prisoners were again manacled and told to prepare for a journey. Lucky chatted in Italian to one of the guards and asked where they were being taken. "Napoli," said the man. They were herded into a train and were amused to see so many guards accompanying them.

"It must be a whole army company," observed Pritchard.

"They must think we're pretty dangerous," said Deane-Drummond, holding up his wrists, "even with this lot on."

"We ought to take it as a compliment," said Pexton. "They must think we were recruited out of hell."

As they jolted and swayed on the journey, the guards in Paterson's compartment indulged in a habit of spitting on the floor every few minutes. After a time the lieutenant could stand it no longer. He pointed to a notice which said "*Non sputare*." "Stop spitting, you filthy beasts," he shouted. They did not understand his words, but they got his meaning and tried to curb the habit, not altogether successfully.

It was cold, dark and raining when, after an uncomfortable journey lasting several hours, they arrived at Naples. Transportation of prisoners, either Italian or enemy, in medieval-style chains was a not unfamiliar sight in Fascist Italy. But passengers and railway staff on the station platform and later civilians in the streets gazed in amazement at the British prisoners. These were not the usual hangdog files shambling along under the weight of their shackles. They were erect and proud. So far as they were able under the weight of iron, they marched rather than walked, with one of their number calling the step. And they laughed as they purposely clanked their chains, trying to make as much noise as possible.

At their head marched a man wearing the same uniform as the rest – a khaki battledress that was unfamiliar to the Italians. Again he alone was spared the indignity of manacles. But no less than six soldiers with rifles and bayonets flanked the tall figure.

The guards answered the queries of bystanders, and the news spread like a flame through the watching crowd. They were British. *Paracadutisti*. They had jumped out of aeroplanes. They had caused dreadful explosions. They were "mad Englishmen". They were "the English desperadoes". The prisoners sensed alarm as well as excitement in the crowd and some concern among their captors, and from what they heard in the days that followed, the three interpreters – Lucky, Nastri and Picchi – learned that further similar raids by the British were expected.

Their passage through the dimly lit and malodorous streets brought them to a large stone building surrounded by high walls. It was a civilian jail, the one to which Daly and his men were also taken. There they were placed in cells, six men to each, and left with the information, given by the guard in broken English, that they would all soon be shot. This threat was repeated many times during their stay in the jail.

The cells were filthy. In the corner of each a lavatory overflowed and covered the floor with human excreta.

Interrogators arrived at the prison, and each day the commandos were lined up outside a room and called in one by one. Always the questioning ended with the threat that the next day at 6 a.m. they would face a firing party. The execution promise was repeated so often that the men began to refer to it light-heartedly among themselves as "the six o'clock parade". When a man rejoined his comrades after a spell of interrogation, he was asked jocularly. "Are you for the dawn parade tomorrow as well?" It was obvious to the men that the Italian authorities viewed their raid most seriously, as a criminal act rather than a military operation. But as time went on, they did not take the threat of execution seriously.

One day Lance-Corporal Jones looked out of the barred window of his cell on to a courtyard. If the threat were ever fulfilled, he thought, that was where it would take place. But from that time he never believed that any of them would meet the promised fate. The whole idea, he decided, was preposterous, too theatrical, too much like a scene from a fictional film.

Harry Pexton was confident that, after the nightmare trek over the mountains, the worst experience of his life, he could not believe that it would end facing a firing squad. From the window of his cell he could see Mount Vesuvius. It was an impressive sight, rather beautiful in the distance, its thin spiral of smoke rising perpetually from its summit. It was somehow comforting.

Sergeant Clements spoke convincingly as continually he voiced his view of the situation. "The six o'clock parade? It's a farce. It'll never come to that. Why, they haven't got the guts. It's just a ploy to try to make us talk." He helped considerably to maintain morale among the men.

There was one man, however, who could not share his optimism. That was Picchi, the little Italian-British civilian who had volunteered to accompany the troop on the raid as an interpreter, the man who had not needed to take part at all. He had good reason to be pessimistic: he was a naturalized British subject, but he had been born in Italy, and apart from his knowledge of Italian, he had all the physical characteristics of his race.

Deane-Drummond became aware that Picchi was in a depressed condition and tried to cheer him up.

"It's no good," said Picchi. "They'll find out who I am. I don't see how they can fail."

"I don't see why they should," said the lieutenant. "Not if you stick like glue to the official story – that you are a free Frenchman in the British Army. Remember, don't try to say you are British by blood because you do look European rather than British. But insist you are really French. Honestly, I don't think they can prove a thing."

"Thank you," said Picchi wistfully. "But it looks black to me. I'm sure they already sense I'm Italian – and therefore a traitor in their eyes. I'll do my best in the way you suggest. But I think I've had it."

Clements was a cheer-leader among the men in another sense. "We're the first paratroopers. That means we're something very special in the British Army. As long as we're prisoners, we must never lose our pride. The British race is the finest in the world, so we must never allow any thought but that we are superior to these Iti bastards."

The three interrogators tried various ploys to gain information. Deane-Drummond, for instance, was told by the chief questioner that he was commandant of the prisoner-of-war camp in which they would be imprisoned, and all he wanted was a few details for the Red Cross. All they got out of him was: "My army number is 71076, my rank is lieutenant and my name is Deane-Drummond – and you can expect nothing else." He repeated this endlessly.

They told Paterson they were officers of the Questura, the secret police. "It is a matter of routine that we interview all prisoners. We have to have answers for the record, you understand. When did you leave England and where were you trained?"

Paterson gave his name, rank and number. They offered him a glass of wine. He refused it.

They asked other questions in an affable manner, received the same reply and returned to the first one. "When did you say you left England?"

"I didn't say. I've told you I'm allowed only to give my name, rank and number. I'm afraid you'll have to be satisfied with that."

"You have been caught making war on the civilian population, committing acts of sabotage, and in Italy that is punishable by death," they threatened. "But if you co-operate, you can avoid execution."

"Balls," said Paterson.

Jowett's answers were confined to name, rank and number except when the interrogators greatly desired to know who fired first prior to their capture on the hillside. "A whole company was shooting at us for several minutes before we replied with a single shot," he said. The same reply was given by all those who had been in Jowett's party.

Asked what make of engine was fitted to the aircraft from which they parachuted, several of the men answered unsmilingly: "Crosse and Blackwell." The name of the British tinned-food company was accepted seriously and gravely written down. Asked what type of aircraft dropped them, one man replied: "A Guinness Two-Three." The pen of the interrogator noted that too. Asked the same question, another said: "A Heinz 57." Told one of his colleagues had said a Guinness Two-Three, he said: "The planes were a mixed bag. Mine was a Heinz 57." This was also recorded on paper.

Questions sought to establish whether the party had landed in civilian clothes and changed into uniform after carrying out their act of sabotage. This was obviously a dangerous question, and all insisted that they had descended from the planes in uniform. One man said: "How the hell could we jump with a suitcase in our hands?"

Several times the interrogators told them: "If we find you have behaved like gangsters, I can promise you that you will be treated like gangsters."

Members of the guard who took them each day from their cells to the question room constantly forecast their early death by shooting. To the consternation of the guard, the prisoners took those statements with a light-hearted calmness, though the commandos were not always as optimistic as they appeared. On one occasion they told their captors: "Our Mr Churchill has sworn that for every one of us executed twenty Italian prisoners in British hands will die." After repeating this many times, the paratroopers began to believe that it was in fact a possibility that Churchill might send such a message to the Italian authorities.

It was repeatedly suggested to Corporal Julian by the interrogators that he looked like an Italian. "Your correct name is Giuliano," they insisted.

"I'm Welsh, a member of one of the Celtic races of Britain," he replied. "My name is Julian, and far from being what you say, I don't even happen to like the Italians."

If they thought Julian looked Italian, they could not have failed to be suspicious about Picchi and perhaps to a lesser extent Nastri.

"But you know there is at least one Italian in your party," they said. "You can't deny that."

"There's one I know who *speaks* Italian, but he's a British soldier. You speak English, don't you, and you're not English? In any case there couldn't possibly be an Italian in our party – no Italian would have the guts to jump out of an aeroplane with a parachute."

The interrogator glared. "Wait and see what we have in store for you at six in the morning," he snapped. Then, turning to the guard: "Take him away."

Invited to state what job they had in civilian life before joining the Army, one man said: "I was a hangman. They thought I'd be OK to hang from a parachute." Another light-heartedly said he had been a bookie's runner.

"Ah, you were an athlete?" was the response.

"Yes, I had to be able to run like hell," smiled the trooper.

They thought it surprising how seriously their answers were taken when they felt able to give some innocent ones instead of the usual. "I can't answer."

For poor Picchi, however, the interrogations were a nightmare. From the start he never had a chance. Extremely Italianate in looks, and his English not quite perfect, he was a sitting duck for their tricky questions. In addition, the fact that the brave and sensitive fellow was most anxious that none of his comrades should suffer because of him did not assist his performance before his questioners. He had lived in Britain for twenty years and was a naturalized Briton. But to the Fascist interviewers he was still an Italian. And a traitor.

The last night he spent with his comrades followed an unusually long session in the interview room, from which he returned in a state of utter dejection. He sat in a corner of the cell, staring fixedly in front of him, shivering with the cold.

"Try to get some sleep," Lance-Corporal Jones told him. "There aren't enough blankets to go round, but lie down next to me and share the one I've got. It won't help for you to get too cold."

Jones talked to him until he appeared to be asleep and then doubled the blanket over him, himself lying uncovered. The corporal woke about 2 a.m. The moonlight filtered through the window, and he could see that Picchi was jerking and mumbling as though dreaming. Jones touched his shoulder and asked what was wrong. Picchi opened his eyes.

"Are you all right?" repeated Jones.

"Yes, I'm all right," replied Picchi.

"But, you don't feel too good, eh?" said Jones gently.

"No, I think it is all up with me. They know who I am."

Jones spent the night trying to comfort the little Italian. It did not matter what his nationality was, said the corporal, because he was a British soldier and there was nothing they could do to him.

"A civilian in uniform, you mean, not a soldier," said Picchi. "They've guessed that too."

"If that's the way you want to put it then. But the British uniform will protect you. They wouldn't dare." As he spoke, Jones knew there was no hope for him.

Picchi was under great emotional strain, and Jones put his arm about the fellow's shoulder. "Never mind. Go to sleep. It won't be so bad as you think. It damn well can't be. Remember what Clem keeps saying. They wouldn't dare."

At last sleep came to the London hotel worker, the civilian who had never needed to be there, the former Italian who hated the Fascists and had not needed to volunteer his services for a raid of particular peril for him. But he did not rest properly, and Jones, watching over him continually, patted his shoulder and comforted him.

They came for Picchi the next morning and took him away. None of the paratroopers ever saw him again. It was learned later that on a cold Sunday morning he was executed, his back placed to a firing squad in the belief that he was a traitor to Italy.

CHAPTER TWENTY-TWO

A narrow escape

Following Picchi's execution there was a great deal of worry among the commandos that the true identity of Trooper Nicol Nastri might be discovered. If so, he would undoubtedly share the fate of the tragic banqueting-manager from a London hotel.

Nastri had also been born in Italy. That he had gone to live in London as a child with his parents and was a British subject would not, they now knew, save him from Italian Fascists bent on revenge. He had acted as an interpreter on the raid, in his case in addition to his military duties, for he was a trained soldier. He was known to have been speaking fluent Italian at the time of his party's capture. His Army Book, when produced, showed him as Trooper John Tristan, but when he was surrounded by Italians, his comrades noted how like them he was in appearance. No one was sanguine about his chances.

Having proved that Picchi had been born and lived for many years in Italy, and having summarily disposed of him, the interrogators turned their full attention to Nastri. They gave him a rough time, but the cheerful cockney character gave a good account of himself. In his case he had lived in London from childhood and spoke English like an Englishman, with a cockney accent that had been acquired naturally over the years. In answer to questions, he was able to talk freely and accurately about London and British affairs over the space of at least two decades. He stuck to his guns that he was a British subject and a soldier in that country's army. They were unable to shake him with any question about the British Army.

There was, however, one remaining danger – the name on his Army pay book, and it might have been wiser if a different pseudonym had been used for him for the raid. The secret police toyed with the name Tristan, and it did not take them long to rearrange the letters until they came up with an Italian name with which they were familiar – Nastri. Many families bearing the name were visited by the *Questura*, and eventually they called upon an aunt of the trooper who lived near Naples. Unaware that she might be placing a relative in danger, she admitted under questioning that one of her brothers had gone to live in Britain many years ago. Yes, her brother had a small son, whom he had taken with him.

The next day Trooper Nastri was taken from his cell and told to accompany an officer to one of the gates leading to the courtyard. Standing there with two soldiers was his aunt. There was no doubt in Nastri's mind who she was, for he had accompanied his parents on a visit to Italy shortly before the outbreak of war and on that occasion had met her.

Would she recognize him? Fortunately his aunt had realized there was something mysterious afoot when, following the visit by the police, she was taken to the jail. The old lady had good eyesight. She recognized her nephew from a distance. What was he doing in an Italian jail in British Army uniform? She was also highly intelligent and had heard the news about the "English desperadoes".

Nastri was determined not to recognize her and prayed that she would make no move. They walked him slowly past her. Not a glimmer of recognition passed between them. His relative was taken to the interrogation room, and then he was marched in – to find her sitting on a chair.

One of the interviewers pointed to the trooper. "Do you know this man?" he demanded of her.

Nastri stood to attention staring at the wall above her head, his face expressionless.

"No," said his aunt.

"You have never seen him before?"

"Never."

"I do not think you tell the truth. Is he your nephew?"

"Nephew? Which nephew?"

"The one who went to live in England with your brother, who forsook our country. Could he be that nephew?"

"Never in this world. That nephew is, I know, a sickly man, always ill. This is a healthy man. Anyway, I've never seen him before." She spoke volubly in Italian, rising from the chair. Then she walked across to confront Nastri, shook her fist in his face and shouted: "*Bastardo!* English soldier. *Bastardo!*"

Never did Nastri love his aunt more than at that moment, and from that time all questions about his nationality ceased.

The third interpreter, Flight Lieutenant Lucky, was never accused of being an Italian. His appearance was British, as was his demeanour, and the English-speaking interviewers recognized his speech as that of a born Englishman with a different accent from that of cockney 'Trooper Tristan', though they had to admit that Tristan's also appeared natural. They accepted at once that Lucky was a British airman who was a linguist (in fact he spoke many languages fluently) and that he had joined the raid in case in an interpreter might be necessary.

Probably because he spoke their language so well, they even showed him some friendliness, and taking advantage of this he asked for permission to leave the jail under escort to buy washing and shaving kit, new underclothes, pyjamas and other necessities for the imprisoned officers and men. He was successful also in securing some other privileges for his comrades and was able to tell them that, as they had come in aeroplanes, they were considered to be Air Force prisoners, and the officers were to be removed for the remainder of their stay in Naples to a nearby Italian air base. His news proved to be correct, and when he and the other six officers were taken there, they were given a room in the officers' quarters and excellent meals and allowed to bath and to exercise on the roof.

In command of the base was a Colonel Montalba, who treated them with kindness and consideration. Later, when Montalba learned that the paratroopers at the jail were being finger-printed and photographed like criminals, he made representations to the prison governor that such records should be destroyed.

The men remaining at the jail were not so lucky regarding washing-facilities. Day after day the NCOs informed the guard that it was essential for the men to have a bath. For some time their requests were ignored. But on a bitterly cold day their guards brought a huge old iron tub into the courtyard and filled it with ice-cold water. Pointing to it, they said: "This what you ask for." They laughed raucously at their joke, not believing that the British prisoners would use the tub. But not one of the commandos was prepared to lose face before their captors, who were astonished to see every one strip, jump into the icy water and splash, shout and laugh.

The paratroopers, blue-lipped and shuddering, said to each other: "Bloody hell, this is the bravest thing we've ever done."

The guards said: "They are quite mad. The English are known to be mad."

They had been known to make the same statement when they had found the paratroopers playing cards for "half a mountain" or "the hair from the next hair-cut". But before the paratroopers were moved from the jail, they had gained the respect of the Italians.

Harry Boulter, his fractured ankle improving, rejoined his comrades at this prison. He warned them that, when he had been searched some of the articles hidden in his uniform had been discovered and confiscated, and the men took most of the Italian paper money from the lining of their tunics and hid it in straw, in holes in the walls and on window ledges in their cells. One man screwed a note into a ball and placed it in his ear, while another managed to get one behind his eyelid. About a quarter of the money they left in their tunics, and when they were searched, their captors were satisfied with what they found. The money they had hidden was used later to buy shaving materials and much-needed fruit and chocolate.

During the search of his kit Corporal Fletcher, much to his annoyance, was relieved of a bottle of liniment, which he always carried for toning up his muscles, a habit he had formed in civilian life when he had been a part-time professional footballer.

After three weeks at Naples the officers and men of 'X' Troop were told that they were to be taken the next day to Campo di Concentramento 78 at Sulmona, a top-security prisoner-of-war camp in mountainous country.

The train which took them passed through desolate country. It looked much the same as that over which they had slogged in their vain attempt to reach the coast and freedom. There were snow-capped peaks and thick pine woods, then an area of vineyards, and at last the train pulled in to a small uplands station bearing the name Sulmona. It was dusk and rain was falling – just such a night as that on which they had been introduced to Naples.

Waiting to escort the prisoners on a five-mile march to the camp was a large detachment of *carabinieri* commanded by a colonel. Their guards were immaculately dressed in what appeared to be their best uniforms, as though they had been informed that the prisoners they were to meet were very important ones. But the *carabinieri* were not to remain smart for long on the wet, muddy route they had to take, and before long they were grumbling aloud at their unpleasant task. The prisoners, however, sang as they marched, splashed the uniforms of their guards and laughed at their discomfiture.

They joined many other Allied prisoners of war in a camp covering about a dozen acres and surrounded by a high brick wall and three outer fences of barbed wire. The place was divided into a number of compounds, in all of which armed guards in high cabins overlooked the area twenty-four hours a day, using brilliant searchlights at night.

In this fortress in the hills, from which escape seemed impossible, Britain's first paratroopers to go into action were to remain as prisoners of war for a long time.

CHAPTER TWENTY-THREE

Escape

Conditions in Campo di Concentramento 78 at Sulmona were severe. There was a degree of comfort, though little food, in the section built for captured officers, who included some RAF and Royal Navy men, Greeks from the war in Albania, and French, and there were compounds for exercise.

The sergeants and other men of the party were put in a special small compound and at nights locked in a hut, where they annoyed the guard by singing loudly, for which they were punished by having their rations cut. Often they would be awakened in the night and kept standing outside in the cold while the hut was searched. They refused to salute Italian officers and were constantly placed in the camp prison.

Later, after visits by Red Cross representatives, they were moved into the main compound for other-rank prisoners. This was an improvement, but after a few months the food was cut down further to a near-starvation level of $6\frac{1}{2}$ pounds a week, and to provide a meal a day the meat, macaroni and greens had to be minced together. There was a little bread but never potatoes. "I saw men bury their faces in their pillows at night and cry for want of food," Sergeant Lawley recalls.

In their letters home they were able to send information of some military value by using a code they had learned at Mildenhall in England before the raid took place. In return they received maps, money and messages hidden in food parcels.

There was soon talk of attempting to break out of the prison, and Major Pritchard formed an escape committee to co-ordinate individual ideas on the subject.

After about six months of imprisonment, Captain Lea and Lieutenant Deane-Drummond notified him that they were hatching an escape plot which they thought might work, given a little luck. During escorted walks round the inside perimeter, they had noted a place at one end of the camp where the ground level changed. Due to this there was a break in the barbed wire, so that, apart from stay wires at an angle, a small part of the wall was free of obstruction. For the same reason there was a small gap in the outer barbed wire. Not unaware that this was a weak place in their protective wall, the camp authorities had fixed an electric lamp at this point which was kept lit at night. The two officers realized that an escape bid would necessitate this light being extinguished. But that would have to be effected in a clever manner if suspicions were not to be aroused.

For a month Pritchard and his committee discussed the possibilities of an escape over the wall at this point. No more than two could expect to get over safely, and much to their delight it was decided that these should be Lea and Deane-Drummond as it was their idea. The final plan was that the two would boldly approach the wall with a ladder, pretending to be civilian electricians, a number of whom were employed in the camp, and unscrew the bulb.

They begged and borrowed a number of articles of civilian clothes from other prisoners, who had bought them at some stage before being sent to Sulmona. But these were not enough, and the two officers made garments to supplement them from scraps of cloth handed over to them. Pritchard handed over to Deane-Drummond a civilian raincoat he had bought while in Naples. Sergeants Lawley and Clements collected every piece of spare wood they could find and constructed a rough ladder. An oilskin package containing maps, money and a small compass was to be stuck with plaster to the leg of each escapee.

Lea and Deane-Drummond decided that, once over the wall, they would split up and run in opposite directions to make it more difficult for pursuers if their escape were immediately discovered. Lea's plan was to hop goods trains up the length of Italy, Deane-Drummond's to walk for three nights over the mountains to Pescara and thence join queues at railway ticket offices and take trains to the Swiss border.

"I'd be spotted as an alien at a ticket office because of my fair hair," said Lea.

Flight Lieutenant Lucky coached them in the use of a few Italian phrases they might require. One was how to ask for a railway ticket in Italian, and both became as near perfect as possible in their pronunciation.

At last the preparations were completed. They were ready to go. The end of 1941 was approaching, and the evening of 7th December was chosen for the attempt.

At 9 p.m. Lea and Deane-Drummond went to the NCOs' compound to pick up the ladder from Lawley and Clements. The time had been chosen carefully so that they would have almost two hours before the moon appeared, darkness being essential in order to pass themselves off as camp workers.

They took possession of the ladder, thanked the sergeants for their whispered good-luck wishes and prepared to cross the French compound in order to reach the selected part of the outer wall. They got no more than a couple of paces before they had to halt and fade into the shadows. A *carabinieri* patrol stood talking in the middle of the compound! If they went on, they would have to pass close to the group of men, who seemed to be engaged in a joke-telling session. A glance at the two officers from close quarters and the game would be up.

For more than an hour the patrol remained while the two kicked their heels impatiently. At last the *carabinieri* dispersed. The compound was empty. But the first gleams of moonlight were appearing. Very soon the light of the moon would be full. The attempt would have to be postponed. Disconsolately they returned the ladder to the sergeants and went back to their quarters.

The following night brought them better luck. The French compound was deserted, and they passed through it to the vicinity of their target – the lamp shining brightly in the darkness. In addition to the ladder they carried coils of flex and electric light bulbs and successfully passed themselves off as electricians whenever they came into a sentry's view.

They worked quickly then. Deane-Drummond climbed up the ladder. His hand was reaching out for the bulb when, from some distance, a sentry shouted. The lieutenant thought it sounded more like a query than a challenge. "*Lampada*," he called back by way of explanation and sighed in relief as the sentry smiled and raised a hand with the thumb inverted. The two escapees hoped the sentry's sign indicated disgust at the quality of the lamp. Pinning their hopes on its not occurring to the sentry that it seemed strange to be changing a lamp that was already shining brightly, the two officers proceeded with their work. It certainly seemed strange that the Italian onlooker gave so little thought to the matter, the only possibility, they imagined, being that he thought the lamps were nearing the end of their life and were being renewed.

Deane-Drummond unscrewed the bulb, pretended to select another from a satchel and then screwed it half back so that it was not lit. Then he descended half-way back down the ladder and stepped onto the top of the wall, signalling for Lea to join him.

They had planned to draw up the ladder after them, place it at the other side of the wall and dispose of it when they were over. They thought that, with no light from the lamp, this would be possible. The moon would not be up for an hour. But even in starlight the sentry's eyes were sharp, and this new operation with the ladder signalled danger to him. He shouted excitedly to the nearest high cabin.

Deane-Drummond had had time to reach the point where they could drop down, and he got his legs over the wall. But Lea, who had just scrambled onto the wall, had not. Half of Deane-Drummond's body was below the other side of the parapet, Lea's in full view atop the wall when they were caught in the sudden beam from the searchlight in the cabin. Almost simultaneously the firing started.

Deane-Drummond hung from the wall, clinging for a moment with his hands before he dropped. Lea had not much time. He just jumped.

The sentry was using a type of bullet which disintegrated into fragments. One small piece grazed Deane-Drummond's cheek. Lea got a full load in his leg, and when he reached the ground, he knew he had been hit. His legs crumpled, and he could not rise. Deane-Drummond turned, pausing for a moment. Lea knew that he must keep his wound from him, otherwise he would return to help.

"I'm OK," he shouted. "Get on with it Tony, for God's sake – I'm off the other way."

Thus, believing that all was well with Lea, the lieutenant made off. The captain heard his footsteps fading in the distance before he lost consciousness.

When he came to, bells were clanging, men were shouting and he was being carried back into the camp where he was given immediate medical attention. An artery had been severed, and he had lost a good deal of blood. After first-aid treatment he was taken to a hospital at Sulmona and later returned to the camp, where he was surprised to find that he neither lost any privileges nor received a reprimand — probably because the wound had almost cost him his life.

Having got over the wall and through the barbed wire, Deane-Drummond evaded search-parties from the prison. He circled the camp and began the ascent of the mountain behind it, travelling due north by the pole star. Short of the snowline, he sat down and ate some chocolate from a small stock of food he carried and a lump of snow in lieu of a drink. During the day he lay up in a clump of juniper bushes and at night took to a main road in the direction of Pescara. The next day he hid in a bed of leaves in a dry culvert running under the road.

When Pescara was in sight, he was able to delay his entry until the last moment because Lucky had stolen a railway timetable at Milan from the *colonelo*'s office while acting as spare interpreter. Deane-Drummond knew therefore the time his train would leave. But his civilian clothes were somewhat disreputable, the new raincoat muddied and torn. He entered the railway station and walked boldly to the ticket office. Anxious that his appearance might bring suspicion on him, he asked for a ticket to Milan with as confident a voice as he could muster and using the phrases he had been taught by Lucky.

The clerk eyed him closely. Deane-Drummond thought the best thing to do was smile as affably as possible. The clerk returned the smile, made a gesture with one hand and a comment in Italian which the refugee failed to understand. He hoped the man was saying something like "Have you been sleeping in a pigsty?" His only reply was to extend the palms of his hands in a gesture of resignation and add a smile for good measure. The ticket was handed to him, and he passed over money in Italian notes.

Sitting in the train, he felt a good deal safer, though anxious for the engine to begin pulling out. But just before the train began to move, two *carabinieri* flung open the door of his compartment and stepped in. This, thought Deane-Drummond, was it. They stared at him. He returned the look, outwardly calm, inwardly alarmed. Then they gave him a word of greeting, sat down beside him, opened newspapers and began to read. It took the lieutenant quite half an hour to reassure himself that they were passengers on the train like himself. Nor did he feel safe so long as the journey lasted, and he prayed that they would not try to engage him in conversation, for his lack of knowledge of the language would soon be discovered.

When the train stopped at Bòlogna, he bought for 9 lire from a platform trolley a cardboard box containing a roll, a leg of chicken, an orange and a piece of cheese. He never enjoyed a meal more before or since, despite the presence of the *carabinieri*.

At Milan he took a train to Como, where he alighted and walked out of the town. It was just a comfortable walk to the Swiss frontier now. As he swung along the road, he prayed that his luck would hold.

He was only a few miles from the border, already congratulating himself, when down the road towards him marched a squad of soldiers. Perhaps, like the *carabinieri* in the train, they would ignore him, take him for an Italian civilian.

They were almost past him when the NCO in charge of the party halted the men, who formed a circle around him. The NCO demanded to see his papers. There was nothing for it but to comply. The papers had been forged in the camp at Sulmona. The picture purporting to be of him had been taken from a magazine and treated to make it appear glossy like a photograph. The NCO looked several times from the picture to Deane-Drummond's face. The refugee knew that he did not present a remarkable likeness to the picture, and he was not surprised that the Italian was not satisfied.

They marched him to a post at the Italian side of the frontier, where he made an attempt to pose as a German without convincing the Italians. The frontier post had been furnished with a list of wanted men. This contained the name of Lieutenant Deane-Drummond and a good description of him. His bid for freedom was over.

It was particularly disappointing to have been caught so near to the frontier. Judging by the length of time it took to reach the Italian post, he reckoned that he must have been within a couple of miles of his target when he was stopped. He asked an officer to state, for his interest, why the soldiers had stopped him. "It was because of your ragged appearance, particularly your dirty boots," was the reply.

He was taken to an officers' prison at Montalbo to undergo thirty days solitary confinement for attempting to escape and was then returned to Sulmona.

In the meantime Flight Lieutenant Lucky had made an escape attempt, using a makeshift ladder at a different – and darker – part of the wall. In his case he had to use stolen wire-cutters, and as it was a silent night, the sounds he made were heard. He dropped to the ground outside the wall but did not get much further than Lea had done before a patrol rushed out and grabbed him. During Deane-Drummond's absence Pritchard and Paterson had also been accused of having organized escapes. The accusations were correct.

Deane-Drummond returned to Sulmona to find that these three, together with four French officer prisoners, had been transferred to a special camp built near Pisa for dangerous prisoners. He was sent there to join them.

This camp was built round an old monastery. Each monk's cell was used to house two prisoners. But part of the building was still occupied by Italian monks, and Lucky made good use of this by pretending to be a Roman Catholic and requesting confession with one of them. By this means he was able to study from the outside the building in which they were imprisoned. After several visits to 'confession' he informed his friends that one of their own cells lay right next to a deserted passage. "It is narrow and dark," he told them, "and no one ever appears to use it."

The eight officers from Sulmona – four British and four French – began to dig a hole under the wall of this cell. It was a long job, and they had to use all their wits to keep evidence of their work hidden whenever the cell was visited. Unfortunately their excavation was discovered before it was completed.

Some time later, when the Italian excitement over this had died down, Deane-Drummond thought up yet another idea for escaping. He feigned illness and was transferred to a hospital in Florence, taking with him the civilian clothes he had used previously in a suitcase which was never inspected. The room in which he lay was guarded by *carabinieri*, but one night he managed to open the window without attracting attention. He stepped out onto a narrow ledge high above the ground and edged his way along it until he could enter a lavatory by another window. From there he crept downstairs and found a ground-floor window which he could open quite easily.

It was not until the next morning that his absence was discovered, and by then he was in a train travelling towards the Swiss border. He changed trains several times, and at last he was on the final lap, walking towards the frontier. Using the tiny compass with which each member of the troop had been furnished, located within the back of his collar stud, he kept away from all roads.

This time his luck held. At last, successfully avoiding border posts, he burrowed under the frontier wires and crawled through to freedom – eventually to take further active part with the British Army in a number of theatres of war, including the invasion of France and the push into Germany.

CHAPTER TWENTY-FOUR

"A legendary figure"

Of those remaining at the Sulmona concentration camp, Jowett was no less busy planning an individual break-out. One of his first ideas had been to jump off the roof of one of the buildings into a ditch outside the wall. But Clements, with whom he discussed this, argued against that particular scheme. He told Jowett he believed that too much noise would be made before he began cutting his way through the barbed wire fences beyond.

Lucky's abortive attempt was still in their minds, and all it had done for him was to get him transferred to a camp of even higher security. So time passed while Jowett impatiently kicked his heels. Eventually, however, he noted that repairs were being effected near the French compound, and during this operation the lights could not be switched on there at night. Advantage of this must be taken, he decided.

Clements and Lawley helped him over the wall without being spotted, and he cut his way through the barbed wire with a pair of pliers that had been stolen and secreted. He managed to make one train journey towards Switzerland but was recaptured while changing to another train and returned to the camp.

In the summer of 1942 the sergeants and men of 'X' Troop began to dig an escape tunnel. They excavated downwards inside one of their huts for fifteen feet and then began a tunnel to pass under the wall, the perimeter barbed wire fences and a road which encircled the camp. To facilitate this, they had asked for and been granted permission to dig up part of their compound and construct a garden. This gave them a place to dump the earth they excavated though great care had to be taken. As time passed, all seemed to be going well, and they began to entertain hopes of escaping. They had been working hard on this operation for three months, and their tunnel extended for 172 feet, when their secret was discovered and their hopes were dashed. After that, regular, careful examinations of their huts prevented a repeat performance.

In 1943 the Allied invasion of Sicily began, followed by substantial landings in Italy and a steady advance north. The Sulmona camp lay in the path of the Allies, and some time before it was overrun, the Italians guarding the prisoners of war began to leave, fleeing north. One day the many prisoners, including those there from 'X' Troop, awoke to find that not a single guard remained. Incredibly they were all free. It was a remarkable sight, they say, to see the prisoners streaming out of the gates and wandering among the foothills.

Many of the guards had been reasonably friendly towards them, and they knew the reason for the guards' retreat out of the camp. Banding together in groups ranging from twos and threes to a score and more, the prisoners camped on the hillsides, returning from time to time to carry out whatever food had been left behind by the camp staff. Some begged food for their supplies from isolated Italian houses, and in most cases this was readily given. It seemed that all they needed to do was remain in the countryside near the camp, subsisting as best they could, until the Allied drive north reached them.

This was a mistaken policy as German troops were on their way south and were keeping an eye open for the prisoners the Italians had deserted. Not all remained in the hope of linking up with the British Army, but many of those who did were recaptured by the Germans, imprisoned first in the more northerly part of Italy and then in POW camps in Germany for the duration of the war.

Among those who set off to try to find the invading British forces were the inseparable Sergeants Clements and Lawley, who first took to the hills and then struck south. After thirty-one days of gruelling marching, climbing eight-thousand-foot-high mountains, receiving help from friendly Italians and evading German troops, they eventually stole through the Nazi lines to come up with units of the British Army at Cassacalenda in October 1943.

The story of their trek in September and October 1943, from the vicinity of Sulmona to find the British Army, is best told by Clements' diary which he wrote each day. These were the entries:

Sunday, Sept 12th: Self, Taff and four others out from the hills to dinner at home of friendly Vittorio. Food and wine wonderful. But Jerry reccy plane sweeping over camp, hills and garden where drinking wine. Got back at once to hiding place in hills to find it deserted. Very cold. No sleep that night.

Monday, 13th: On our reccy of the area collected 53 former fellow prisoners, including Slavs, all of whom I now have to look after. Decide to make our way south. Vittorio pro-British and first-class bloke. Gave us milk and bread to take with us, but he cannot supply any arms. Jerry not here yet but expected any moment. Each managed to get a parcel of food from empty prison camp. Cold at night prevented sleep.

Tuesday, 14th: Jerry arrived about 0900 hours. From hill saw them enter empty prison camp. Some shooting further down hill — we moved further up and many of my party decide to go off in ones and twos, thinking this safer. Eleven Slavs stick to Taff and me. They seem lost without a NCO among them, so we look after them. Crossed in moonlight to forest below La Mejilla.

Wednesday, 15th: Map (sent in food parcel) shows if our invasion began in Scicily then we've wasted a lot of energy wrong way for probable direction our troops. Decide to cross La Mejilla (2795 metres). Can hear sounds of demolition or blasting by Jerries from direction Sulmona. Crossed mountain. Ten miles of downhill agony. Reached water near Letto Palena about midnight.

Thurs, 16th: Reached Letto Palena and found two more Iti friends, Beniamino and Giuseppe. Slept in house. Clean bed. Wonderful. Jerry patrols on road. We have no weapons, keep our heads down. Bought bread, cheese and eggs (money from food parcels). Slavs have deserted us. Don't know why. But Taff and I now on our own and less responsibility.

Fri, 17th: Left LP and arrived Monterodomo at 1700 hours. Grand meal. Alfredo Rossi and family exceptionally good to us. Still can't get any civvy clothing or guns.

Sat, 18th: Good meals all day. Moving tomorrow. Conflicting rumours as to where troops and Jerry are. Good sleep on spring bed.

Sun, 19th: Alfredo's son took us to Civitaluparella, but villagers afraid because Jerry stationed near and patrols expected in village. Dinner of apples, grapes, tomatoes and bread. Other Sulmona ex-prisoners there, all now in civvies. We (in uniform) left and moved on to Fallo, where Pasquale Rassato (82 years old) gave us bread but scared to let us stay as Jerry expected any moment. But he and his son, armed with axe and knife, led us for several kilos towards Rassello. Got bread there but people scared. Went on till midnight towards Castiglione Messer Marino. Tried to sleep in high forest on mountain, but too wet and cold.

Monday, 20th: Very weak. Chest bad. Real struggle to keep marching, particularly climbing. Better food from Iti civvies now, but prison at Sulmona must have taken pretty bad toll on us.

   Reached village at 1930 hours. Found English-speaking couple there, and given bread and cheese. Carried on for Schiavi D'Abruzzi. Hiding off road eating raw eggs and bread when German ambulances passed. Warned by Iti man, wife and daughter that Jerry patrols near Schiavi. Crossed Tragino River. Exhausted. Jerry plane flew over us at 200 ft. Slept in Capanna on straw in outhouse. Bought bread, eggs, cheese and ham in Trevento.

Tues, 21st: On again. When will this trek end? Given fried eggs and bread from very poor family beside Trattura. Halted near S. Lucita. Slept in hay loft.

Wed, 22nd: Rested all day, Just couldn't move, quite jiggered. Slept same place. Boots nearly worn through.

Thurs, 23rd: Set off 0600 hours. Men and women led us by track and road over Bifemo River. Passed Morrone. Intended reach Ripabottome, but feel all in and ill. Turned back with three people to Morrone. Jerry supposed to be at or near. Had meal at Tommassini and slept at Morrone. Women brought some kind of medicine tablets and coffee.

Fri, 24th: Moved down to convent, led by Gina Antonelli after wonderful meal at his house. Couldn't stay there so moved down to Cappella della S. Maria. Five other ex-POWs there, but three moved out to a farm. Giovanni Melfi very poor but grand chap.

Sat, 25th: Many people came to convent to bring us bread, eggs, potatoes, oil and flour.

Sun, 26th: Jerry called. Stayed quiet in chapel. A near do.

Mon, 27th: German column moving N.E. on secondary road from Cassacalenda through Guadalfiera. Borrowed field-glasses to see better but eyes very weak.

[*Tues, 28th*: No entry.]

Wed, 29th: Sound of bombs and guns good way off. Hope our lot advancing.

Thurs, 30th: Heard our lads only 25 kilos away. Then heard it was false alarm. Depressed. Italians ahead of us trying to take us through to Foggia stopped by big company Jerries. Miracle we were not discovered.

Fri, Oct. 1st: Jerry back in Morrone with 14 vehicles and only one mile away. Lie low and hope. Eat chicken given to us.

Sat. 2nd: Jerry still at Morrone. We can't move.

Sun, 3rd: Rumour Jerry evacuated Morrone and Cassacalenda and English patrol arrived at latter but turned back. No confirmation, and heard later Jerry still in strong force around us.

Mon, 4th: Saw with glasses large Jerry force moving north on Cassacalenda secondary road. Many tanks. Our planes bombed during evening north of us.

[*Tues, 5th*: No entry]

Wed, 6th: Rumour our lads only 8 kilos from Cassacalenda. Artillery certainly sounds near.

Thurs, 7th: Columns still moving north night and day.

Fri, 8th: Guns and bombs much clearer. Giovanni has exhausted his supply of oil, potatoes and tomatoes for us.

Sat, 9th: Flares in the east last night.

Mon, 11th: Villagers report having seen many Germans wounded. Jerry taken mattresses and blankets from them.

Tues, 12th: Cassacalenda ridge plastered by our artillery. Jerry destroyed bridge at Guadalfiera and four or five extremely heavy explosions to south and west.

Wed, 13th: Heard our lads have taken Cassacalenda, so returned to convent chapel for some of our belongings. Only 50 yards from it when a woman screamed at us to escape quickly as Jerry patrol had arrived and was waiting for us. Poor woman. Wonder what happened to her? We fled and arrived Cassacalenda 1300 hours. Our troops were there. Green Howards. Wonderful to join them. We moved back to S. Croce di Magliano. Taff says 13 will always be his lucky number now.

Thurs, 14th: Moved from there to Foggia and on to Bartella. Had hair-cut there and feel human again. Listened to British radio for first time for about two years.

Fri, 15th: By lorry to Tarranto. Board boat for home.

Clements and Lawley continued service as paratroopers for the remainder of the war.

Many of the Sulmona prisoners, including most of 'X' Troop, had the misfortune to walk into ambushes set by Nazi troops or to be rooted out of their hiding-holes in the hills. They were soon on their way to Germany.

The men who had been sent to the top-security prison near Pisa, including Pritchard, Paterson and Lucky (Deane-Drummond having successfully escaped), were not left unguarded. Soon after the Allies landed at Sicily, they were put on a freight train on the first leg of a long journey to imprisonment in Germany.

Paterson managed to escape by leaping from the train at night-time and suffering no worse injury than a number of bruises. He joined up with anti-Fascist resistance groups in the Italian mountains, quickly becoming one of their leaders. With them for a long time he waged guerrilla warfare on the German and Italian Fascist forces. In this role his work also included organizing the escape to Switzerland of many

Allied prisoners of war who remained in hiding in Italy. The Italian partisans whom he led looked upon him as a legendary figure.

Eventually, having assisted the escape of as many prisoners as possible and having organized the anti-Fascists in his area into a good fighting force, he made for the border himself and successfully burrowed under the frontier wires into Switzerland. But he was not to remain there for long. While he was enjoying a well-earned rest in Switzerland, the British Special Operations Executive, who had learned about his work with the Italian patriots, asked him to go back across the border into enemy territory to assist the Italian Resistance in the Domodossola sector. If he did so, it would be entirely at his own decision, the SOE impressed on him. They added that he had already done more than might be expected of him in this respect, and if he declined, there would be no hard feelings and they would organize his return to England with an excellent record behind him.

It was a difficult decision for him to make. There had been the Tragino raid, imprisonment at Sulmona and Pisa and a period of great strain with the Italian guerrillas. He was extremely tired. He spent a few hours thinking over what his reply would be. When, later that day, he had a further meeting with SOE's agent in Switzerland, his answer was: "Yes, I'll go back."

He crossed the border and linked up once more with the Italian patriots who were clearing the area of Fascists and Germans. This time he was captured by German troops. A second term of imprisonment began for him at Milan, but later he was freed by the Italian resistance forces.

After the break-up of the Sulmona camp, another member of 'X' Troop also came upon a group of Italian partisan guerrillas and joined forces with them. He was Lance-Corporal Boulter, the man who had broken his ankle landing by parachute in the Tragino valley. He fought with them for nine months before being re-captured by the Nazis and imprisoned in Germany.

The story of the first handful of British soldiers ever to be trained as paratroopers, of the first troop of British airborne commandos to go into action and of what befell them as a result of their drop into the Italian mountains, ends at this point. The rest of the story belongs to what eventually became of the paratroopers, the first of the many, and an evaluation of the Tragino raid and its effects.

CHAPTER TWENTY-FIVE

The importance of the raid

It is interesting to note what happened to the men of 'X' Troop during the remainder of the war. Many remained prisoners, but some managed to continue notable military careers.

Aided by underground organizations, Deane-Drummond reached Gibraltar from Switzerland and sailed by troopship to Britain. He was posted as signals officer to the newly formed 2nd Parachute Brigade and in March 1943 sailed for service in North Africa. The following year he took part in the Arnhem assault and was again taken prisoner, this time by the Germans. Yet again he escaped and rejoined the advancing British Army. During that escape one of the hardships he had to endure was hiding for thirteen days and nights cramped in a wall cupboard in which he had to stand the whole time.

He remained in the Army after the war and retired a few years ago with the rank of major-general.

On returning home after reaching the British Army in Italy after Sulmona, Sergeant Clements was posted to an officer training unit and gazetted full lieutenant in a parachute regiment. He won the MC in the fighting at the Ardennes.

Sergeant Lawley became a company sergeant major in the 13th Battalion Parachute Regiment, took part in the invasion of Normandy and received a certificate signed by Field Marshal Montgomery for "oustanding good service and devotion to duty".

Major Pritchard DSO MBE was promoted after repatriation, but ill health eventually forced him to leave the Army.

Captain Daly remained in the Army and became a lieutenant-colonel.

Captain Lea studied law while a prisoner of war in Germany, was promoted to major after the war but left the Army later for the Bar. He is now a judge.

Flight Lieutenant Lucky was promoted and after the end of hostilities was in command of a transit RAF camp at an airfield in Malta.

Trooper Ross, the youngest man on the raid, who had been described as "Army mad", was commissioned in the Territorial Army after the war.

All have had successful careers in civilian life.

The decision to mount the raid was taken with a number of possible benefits in mind.

From a military point of view an attempt to sabotage the extensive 993-miles-long pipeline system known as the Acquedotto Pugliese was extremely tempting. It carried water through tunnels and over aqueducts by tapping the headwaters of the River Sele at Caposele and supplied two million people in the 'heel' of the country, including Taranto naval base and Brindisi and Bari, which were ports for Italian troops and stores leaving for Mussolini's campaigns in North Africa and against the Greeks opposing him in Albania. Demolition of the chosen aqueduct over the Tragino would cut that supply, and British military authorities estimated that, if the province had to rely on a few local reservoirs – even if only for a month, the resulting confusion and dislocation would have a serious effect on the two Italian campaigns. It was believed that the Italians would be more susceptible to alarm and panic than the Germans.

The organizers of the raid also had other benefits in mind. One was to give operational experience to their as yet tiny paratroop force and test it out. The decision to establish such a force had in the first place caused some considerable controversy, and those who favoured its inception were anxious to vindicate its existence. Another was to use such a raid to demonstrate to the Axis powers and to the world at large that Britain, for the most part confined to its own shores since the complete occupation of Europe by the Nazis, was still very much alive and capable of aggressive action.

What better place than the Italian Apennines existed in the bleak winter of 1940-41, it was asked, to effect such valuable propaganda *at small cost*? In a monetary sense perhaps, but not at small cost to the guinea-pigs, it must be stated.

The paratroopers fulfilled their orders. They blew away a section of the aqueduct, diverting the water supply for a month – the time it took the Italians to repair it.

But for certain misfortunes, the commando troop might have done even better. Due to icing, the jamming of the bomb racks on one of their dropping-planes robbed them of valuable explosives. Nor did they have those from Daly's plane. In addition, those from another plane were released a mile from the target, and not all of them were recovered. Consequently there was less than two-thirds of the load available. It is interesting to surmise that, if Major Pritchard had been in possession of all the explosives and the services of the senior engineer officer, most of the aqueduct might have been brought down and the water supply cut off for a considerable length of time, though this is not to criticize Paterson's performance, which was excellent with the material at his disposal.

One is bound to assume, however, that the wrecking of the aqueduct in itself was of secondary importance in the minds of the organizers. The operation was surely mounted mainly as a test to prove one way or the other just how useful a future large force of paratroopers might be, to discover if it were possible for such troops to strike deeply into enemy territory, reach their objective and operate successfully in difficult terrain. It was essential to determine this before continuing to train many more thousands for this new type of assault, either for sabotage or to transport a force of fighting men rapidly into any theatre of war where in the future they might be required urgently.

Keeping this in mind, the raid was of supreme importance. Firstly, it achieved what it set out to accomplish. Secondly, it was of inestimable value in providing the British High Command with optimism for what lay at all times in the mind – an eventual second front in which the war could be brought back onto European soil. Thirdly, it provided the necessary impetus for many thousands of British soldiers to volunteer for parachuting training. Some time after the raid the British Press were allowed to publish a short, guarded report that the raid had taken place, and when the news was further disseminated, newspapers throughout the world spread the news that Britain possessed a fine force of military parachutists. Apart from bringing in hordes of volunteers to join the British parachute corps, it was excellent propaganda for the Allied war effort.

Though every man who took part ended the operation in captivity, a few finally escaped and one was executed, it must have been considered that the raid either was totally successful or at the very least revealed a strong potential for airborne soldiers in the future conduct of the war. For the British authorities pushed on harder than ever in the production of this type of commando. Even before the second front was launched upon Europe, a formidable number of well-trained paratroop regiments were in existence and had been used in various battles. And when D-Day came, the skies over occupied France were thick with the silvery canopies of invasion.

What effect did the raid have on Italy? In official quarters it was not taken lightly. The Italian military machine felt it had been taken completely off guard, and the feeling existed there that Britain had an entirely new trick up its sleeve, one that amounted almost to a 'secret weapon'. On the civilian side alarm spread throughout the country, even to its most northern parts. People were in a constant state of fear lest the desperadoes of the skies come again, and it became necessary for Italian radio and newspapers to issued propaganda concerning the raid designed to raise general morale.

Radio Roma went so far as to stress that little or no damage had been done to the aqueduct, though the people of Apulia knew better. Nor could bulletins disguise to the rest of Italy the fact that fresh burdens were imposed on them as a direct result of the raid in the way of new and severe regulations. Stringent air-raid precautions came into being, and a new type of observer corps was organized – one that looked not so much for enemy aircraft but for what might float down from them as they flew over. Over a wide area additional guards were posted at strategic points, and the whole district around Monte Vulture was barred to neutrals.

One official Italian statement to the public was: "It has not yet been decided whether to treat these British parachutists as prisoners or spies." Apparently the prisoners were not the only ones to be told this, and it seems evident that the Italian authorities were sufficiently alarmed and angered as to consider the wholesale execution of the troop.

The concern felt in Italy was not lessened by the fact that the aqueduct was repaired as quickly as possible. There was also anxiety that the railway bridge over the Tragino might be unsafe; the gushing water following the explosion, it was believed, might have scoured out the abutments supporting the railway.

There is evidence that Hitler was both fascinated and concerned. He asked for all details of the raid – yet another example of how far-reaching were the effects of Britain's small-scale but first-ever paratroop drop.

In Britain the Prime Minister, Mr Churchill, was delighted with the raid – and not only because it captivated his aggressive spirit. It justified his original idea to form and train soldiers as paratroopers. The first handful of them was now the nucleus for a large force which eventually was to become known as 'the Red Berets', the Parachute Brigades and the Special Air Service.

Because the raid was considered successful, the Parachute School at Ringway in Cheshire went into unlimited production, and the men who succeeded the first trainees were to have things easier. Improved techniques were used, and due to the raid volunteers entered this arm of the service with greater confidence.

Another useful spin-off considered by the authorities following the operation was that it had shown what might be expected to occur in the event of a similar raid on Britain, always known to be a possibility, and therefore useful information had been collected to help counter the dangers of any Nazi penetration of this kind. British newspapers pointed out that it was for just such an eventuality that the Home Guard had been raised, and this part-time force could now be given useful information arising from what had occurred after our own men dropped into Italy.

The Chief of the Imperial General Staff paid a visit to the school. Colonel Rock and Major Lindsay asked that decorations be awarded to those who took part in the raid, and because it was not the rule to give awards to men who were taken prisoner, they had to push their demands strongly in order to gain some medals for their first operative pupils.

"All right then, send some citations," said the military authorities at last. "But the awards cannot be made until the prisoners are freed."

They were made on 20th June 1946.

Major Pritchard received the DSO. Lieutenant Deane-Drummond,

Captain Lea and Second Lieutenant Jowett were given the MC. Lieutenant Paterson was awarded the MC three times over – the first for the raid and two bars for the work he did with the partisan groups in Italy after escaping. Sergeants Clements, Lawley and Durie and Lance-Corporal R.B. Watson gained the MM. Captain Daly, Lance-Corporal Maher and Trooper Nastri were mentioned in despatches in recognition of "gallant and distinguished service in the field". Lance-Corporal Boulter was awarded the MM, not for the raid, as it transpired, but for the part he played for nine months with the Italian partisans following the break up of the Sulmona prison camp.

It is my opinion – and I stress not that of the members of 'X' Troop – that this was a paltry handful of decorations. For a raid such as this, on which all set out cheerfully into completely unknown dangers, in which all showed unusual gallantry and endured so much, surely there should have been more awards. A mere ten out of thirty-five was to my mind unimaginative.

One or two features of the raid remain unusually intriguing.

Why was the submarine never sent to the mouth of the River Sele to assist the escape? That the crippled Whitley ditched there and its survivors were taken prisoner days before the date of the rendezvous does not appear sufficient reason for HMS *Triumph*'s sailing order to be cancelled. Was it because not one single member of the party was ever expected to reach HMS *Triumph* if she sailed there?

In support of such a theory there is one vital sentence given officially by the commanders of their parachute training school when they encountered difficulties in persuading the authorities to grant decorations to Pritchard and members of his party. It was: "If ever soldiers deserve medals, it is these men, because from the moment they jumped from their aircraft, they never had a hope of remaining free."

It is also to be remembered that a supremo saying farewell to them as they left Britain was heard to murmur: "A pity – a damned pity." He well knew that they were embarking on a drop infinitely more dangerous than that other during Hitler's push to France at the start of the war by German paratroopers, who knew that their army was advancing close behind them and in a few days could rescue them. He knew then that for 'X' Troop there was no way back.

Thrown up by research is another question; why was the target chosen sixty miles inland and in a place from which it was difficult or impossible to escape? If an installation not far inland had been chosen, they would have had a far greater chance of reaching the coast. The raid on the Tragino aqueduct was therefore an extraordinarily tough test.

The questions are mine, posed in the light of my research. They have never been asked by the men who took part, none of whom has put forward a single grumble from the day he set out on the adventure – or since. They are all justly proud to have taken part. But they are questions which convince one that, officially as well as in fact, the thirty-five men of 'X' Troop, the paratroop trail-blazers, were indeed guinea-pigs.

In the light of the great successes that came later in the war, including the large-scale airborne operations, the exploit has tended to be overshadowed. But the lifting in recent years of the official wraps on details of wartime missions and operations has enabled the story to be told.

The raid ranks among the most daring of the war, a repeat in modern terms of former exploits – of which Sir Francis Drake's burning of Spanish galleons in Cadiz harbour is one – and it can take its rightful place in the pages of military history.